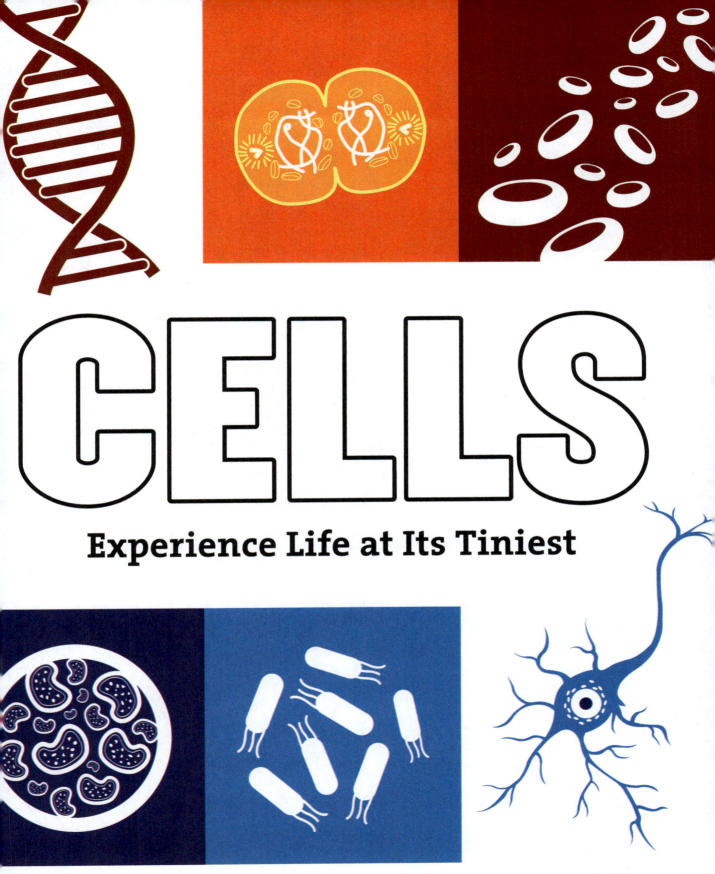

CELLS

Experience Life at Its Tiniest

Karen Bush Gibson
Illustrated by Alexis Cornell

Nomad Press
A division of Nomad Communications
10 9 8 7 6 5 4 3 2 1

This book was manufactured by Marquis Book Printing,
Montmagny, Québec, Canada
July 2017, Job #136265
ISBN Softcover: 978-1-61930-525-0
ISBN Hardcover: 978-1-61930-521-2

Educational Consultant, Marla Conn

Questions regarding the ordering of this book should be addressed to
Nomad Press
2456 Christian St.
White River Junction, VT 05001
www.nomadpress.net

Printed in Canada

Recent science titles in the
Inquire and Investigate series

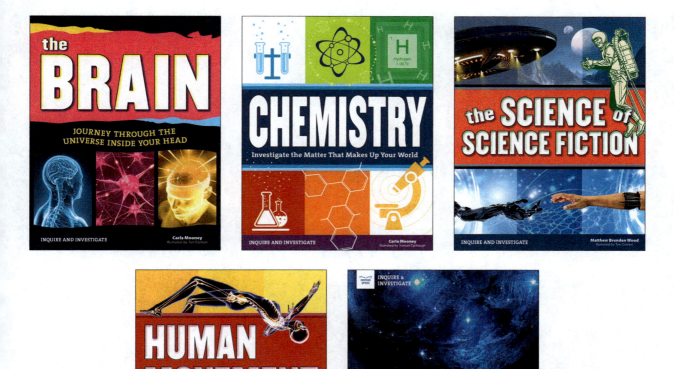

Check out more titles at www.nomadpress.net

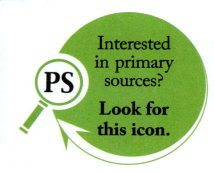

Interested in primary sources?

PS

Look for this icon.

You can use a smartphone or tablet app to scan the QR codes and explore more! Cover up neighboring QR codes to make sure you're scanning the right one. You can find a list of URLs on the Resources page.

If the QR code doesn't work, try searching the Internet with the Keyword Prompts to find other helpful sources.

Cells

Contents

TIMELINE

300s BCE................... Aristotle supports the theory of spontaneous generation and writes widely of animals and nature.

1590s CE................... Hans and Zacharias Janssen invent the first compound microscope.

1663........................ Robert Hooke describes cells when he discovers them in cork.

1665........................ Robert Hooke adds light to a compound microscope and publishes his book, *Micrographia*.

1668........................ Antonie van Leeuwenhoek creates a simple microscope and discovers unicellular organisms.

1675–1679................. Marcello Malpighi publishes several works on the early development of organisms. He is considered by many to be the "father of embryology."

1802........................ Charles-Francois Brisseau de Mirbel proposes that plants are made up of cells.

1832........................ Barthélemy Dumortier observes plant cell division under a microscope. Robert Remak observes cell division in animal cells.

1833........................ Robert Brown discovers the cell nucleus.

1839........................ Matthias Jakob Schleiden and Theodor Schwann propose cell theory.

1842........................ Julius Robert von Mayer publishes the chemical formula for photosynthesis.

1858........................ Rudolf Virchow adds to cell theory by hypothesizing that all cells come from preexisting cells.

1859........................ Louis Pasteur disproves the theory of spontaneous generation.

1866........................ Gregor Mendel publishes his work on genetics and principles of inheritance.

1869........................ Friedrich Miescher discovers DNA.

1881........................ Theodor Engelmann discovers that photosynthesis occurs in the chloroplast.

1886........................ Ernst Abbe and Carl Zeiss invent the modern compound microscope.

TIMELINE

1898............................Camillo Golgi described the Golgi apparatus, an organelle in the cell.

1931............................Ernst Ruska builds the first electron microscope.

1944............................Scientists at the Rockefeller Institute for Medical Research show that all genes have DNA.

1952............................Rosalind Franklin produces the first image of DNA.

1952............................The first human cell line is created.

1955............................The scanning electron microscope (SEM) is invented.

1962............................James Watson, Francis Crick, and Maurice Wilkins receive the Nobel Prize for their discovery of DNA's structure.

1970s.........................Archaea are discovered to be a separate organism from bacteria and receive separate taxonomic classification.

1970s.........................Lynn Margulis publishes work on endosymbiotic theory.

1977............................Frederick Sanger creates a DNA sequencing method.

1981............................Transgenic mice and fruit flies are produced. A mouse embryonic stem cell line is established.

1983............................Thomas Cech and Sidney Altman discover ribozymes.

1990............................The Human Genome Project is started in an effort to map the entire human genome.

1996............................A sheep named Dolly is the first animal to be cloned. Dolly survives for more than six years.

1998............................Mice are cloned from adult stem cells.

1998............................Researchers achieve the first animal genome sequence of the nematode worm.

1998............................The National DNA Index System (NDIS) is created by the FBI.

2003............................The human genome sequence is published.

2012............................A new genetic tool called CRISPR-Cas9 allows for easy editing of sections of DNA.

2016............................GMO labeling legislation is passed, requiring standard labels on genetically modified food.

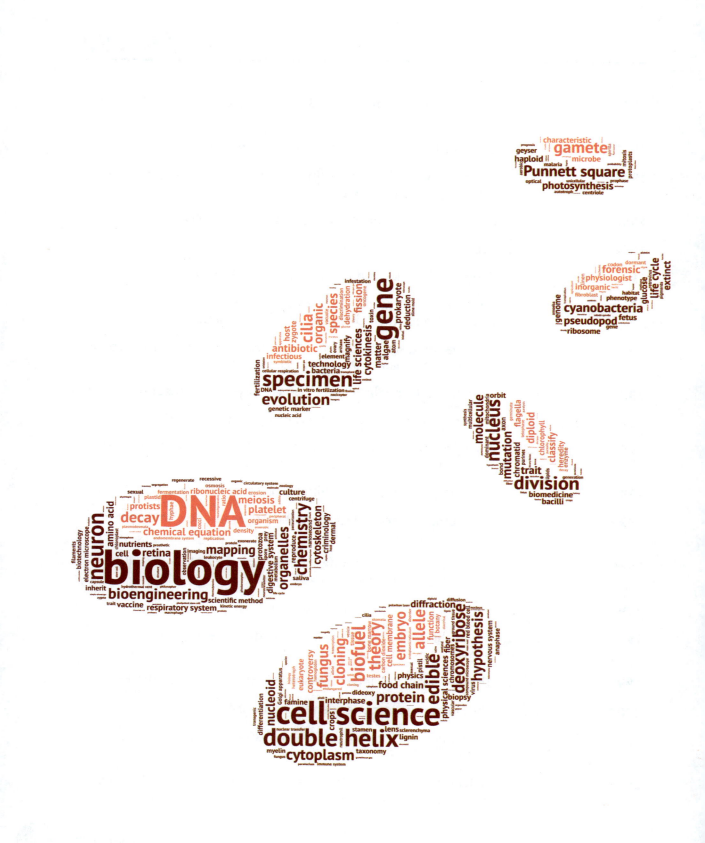

Introduction

Cells Are Life

Why are cells important to the study of biology?

Cells are the building blocks of every form of life. Understanding cells is critical to understanding how living creatures function.

People believe what they can see. This has been true throughout human history. For example, thousands of years ago, people could see that the sun was in a different place in the sky depending on the time of day or time of year. They believed that the sun was moving across the sky.

For thousands of years, this was the accepted explanation, that the sun moved around the earth. Eventually scientists and thinkers proved that it was actually the earth in motion around the sun.

Hundreds of years ago, people noticed that mice appeared in the rags covering cheese and bread. It seemed that the combination of cheese and bread stored in a dark place created mice. This deduction might seem foolish to people today in the twenty-first century. But in the past, people made deductions on what they could see simply with their eyes.

Observations such as this led to a theory called spontaneous generation, which was first suggested by Aristotle (384–322 BCE). Aristotle was a Greek philosopher and scientist who made contributions to many areas, from physics and biology to mathematics and politics. His theory of spontaneous generation stated that some organisms develop from nonliving matter. For example, mice came from bread and cheese. Maggots came from rotting meat. Remember, people tend to believe what they can see!

Not everyone believed in spontaneous generation. Some people suspected that living things were made up of substances similar to what was found in a chemistry lab. However, there was no way to prove it. And from the time of Aristotle, it was understood that science must be observed and measurable to have meaning. It was this belief that led to the scientific method, the process scientists use to perform experiments and make discoveries.

Today, we know that maggots come from eggs that are laid by flies that are attracted to rotting meat. We also know that organisms, which are living things, do not come from nonliving matter. All living organisms, including bacteria, plants, and animals, come from other living things.

[The questions remained:
What is life? How do we prove
something we can't see?]

PRIMARY SOURCES

Primary sources come from people who were eyewitnesses to events. They might write about the event, take pictures, post short messages to social media or blogs, or record the event for radio or video. Why are primary sources important? Do you learn differently from primary sources than from secondary sources, which come from people who did not directly experience the event?

PS

THE INVENTION OF THE MICROSCOPE

Hans Janssen and his son, Zacharias, were eyeglass makers in the Netherlands in the 1590s. They discovered that if they placed two lenses at a distance from each other, the lenses magnified the object being studied. Using this discovery, they created the first compound microscope, a tube with lenses at both ends that could magnify objects up to nine times their size. During the next 50 years, other European scientists improved upon this design until objects could be magnified up to 30 times.

Another man from the Netherlands, Antonie van Leeuwenhoek, was a linen merchant in 1668. He wanted a way to examine super-fine linen fibers, so he began to work on a better lens.

[The lens he developed showed cloth fibers in great detail.]

Van Leeuwenhoek mounted a single lens in a brass holder about 3 to 4 inches long. Specimens mounted on a sharp point in front of the lens were magnified up to 200 times. This Dutch linen merchant had invented the world's first simple microscope. It's called a simple microscope because, unlike the compound microscope, only one lens is used.

It didn't take van Leeuwenhoek long to start looking at other things with his microscope. In a sample of saliva, he saw small organisms moving around. He called them "animalcules." We know them as the one-celled organisms, bacteria. Van Leeuwenhoek might have been the first person to observe bacteria.

Antonie van Leeuwenhoek's first microscope probably looked something like this.

The enthusiastic amateur scientist shared his observations with the Royal Society of London. After his discovery of single-cell organisms was confirmed, he was appointed as a fellow of the Royal Society, the highest honor for scientists. He went on to create about 250 microscopes and he continued studying samples. Among his papers were descriptions of red blood cells, sperm cells, and protists.

While van Leeuwenhoek was creating the simple microscope, British scientist Robert Hooke (1635–1703) was doing his own inventing and observing. With the help of instrument maker Christopher Cook, Hooke created a microscope with a built-in light source. Why do you think Hooke wanted a light source built into the microscope?

Hooke's curiosity for examining items under the microscope was unstoppable. He viewed insects, hair, sand, snow, and plants. When he looked at a piece of cork from a tree, he saw dozens of empty spaces surrounded by walls. Hooke thought the spaces looked like small, plain rooms, like the cells in which monks lived in monasteries. Hooke called the walled spaces "cells." Hooke recorded his observations of samples under the microscope in a book published in 1665 called *Micrographia*.

ROBERT HOOKE

As the person who created the term *cell* to describe the foundation of life, Robert Hooke was perhaps the first expert in cell science. Before becoming a scientist, he was apprenticed as an artist. He was able to use his artistic talent to make scientific drawings of his observations. You can see many of his drawings at this website. Can you see how his understanding of cells developed from his work with the microscope?

🔎 Library of Congress Robert Hooke

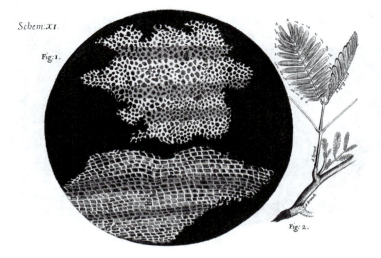

Robert Hooke's drawing of cork. Can you see why he came up with the name "cell" to describe what he saw?

Through cell science, we can understand more than just the outer appearance and behavior of organisms. We can understand why we are the way we are.

WHAT IS A CELL?

Cells are the building blocks of life. Every living thing on Earth is made up of at least one cell. Cells are like members of a community, working together to build something. While cells are essential to our existence, we can't see most cells without a microscope. The period at the end of this sentence is about the size of 50 human cells.

Organisms may contain only a single cell, which is known as unicellular, or be composed of many cells, which is called multicellular. You are a multicellular organism made up of more than 200 types of cells.

Cells vary in how they look and what they do, but they all contain a cell membrane and DNA. They develop and grow. They reach a size limit and then split in two to form two new cells. One cell becomes two, two become four, four become eight, and so on.

[The average human body is made of 37.2 trillion cells. About 50 billion of our cells are replaced each day.]

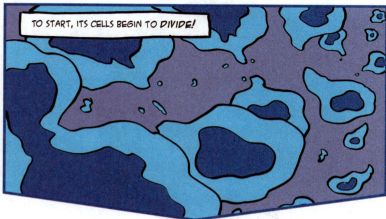

The study of cells is called cell science, also known as cellular biology. Scientists have made great progress in understanding cells. The focus was first on discovering cells and identifying their parts and functions. Today, cell scientists are more likely to focus on specific cell parts and processes than the cell as a whole.

Knowledge about cells cannot be attached to a single person's discovery. Instead, cell science has developed, and continues to develop, from a community of scientists interacting and building upon each other's experiments and theories.

CELL THEORY

Even after microscopes proved the existence of cells, there were people who continued to believe in spontaneous generation. How else could organisms such as mold begin growing in a container of liquid? Where did the mold come from?

In 1859, the French Academy of Sciences offered a prize to whomever could prove or disprove spontaneous generation once and for all. French chemist and microbiologist Louis Pasteur (1822–1895) was interested. You might know Pasteur's contributions to the pasteurization of milk and vaccinations against rabies, but before that, he made a significant discovery in cell science.

In 1859, Pasteur created an experiment with two flasks of broth. One was open. The other had a special S-shaped neck that didn't allow anything to get into the flask. Soon, mold began growing in the open flask, but not in the closed one. When Pasteur removed the S-shaped neck on the second flask, what do you think happened? What could have fallen into the open flask that caused mold to grow on the broth?

THE ROYAL SOCIETY OF LONDON

The Royal Society of London is considered to be the oldest scientific academy in the world. In 1660, a group of learned men that included Great Britain's greatest architect, Christopher Wren, decided a formal group for scientists was needed. The group received approval from King Charles II and became The Royal Society of London for Improving Natural Knowledge.

The society's motto was "Nullius in verba," meaning "Take nobody's word for it." All knowledge had to be verified by experiment. The Royal Society published the discoveries of cell science, as well as work by Isaac Newton and Benjamin Franklin. It sponsored explorations around the world. Do you recognize these members: Charles Darwin, Albert Einstein, Stephen Hawking, and Jocelyn Bell Burnett?

There's one cell that you probably see frequently, and without a microscope. If you've ever cracked an egg, you've seen a cell. An egg yolk is a cell. The largest known cell in the world is the egg cell of an ostrich egg, which is about 6 inches in diameter.

[Pasteur's experiment helped prove that living matter could not simply begin on its own. It had to come from other living matter.]

Scientists Matthias Jakob Schleiden (1804–1881) and Theodor Schwann (1810–1882) both studied plant and animal cells. They discovered many similarities when they compared their scientific notes. In 1839, Schwann summarized their findings by saying that, "We have seen that all organisms are composed of essentially like parts, namely of cells." This was the basis of cell theory, eventually adopted by all scientists.

Cell theory, the foundation of cell science, has the following three components.

- All life is made of one or more cells.
- The cell is the basic structural and functional unit of all organisms.
- All cells come from pre-existing cells.

THE FUTURE OF CELL SCIENCE

The biggest advances in knowledge about cells have occurred in the past 40 years. It's likely that what you're learning today about cell science wasn't known when your parents or grandparents were in school. What do you think your own children will learn? Will new discoveries continue to be made?

Curious people always want to know more, so they move beyond known boundaries and engage in discovery. As scientists have developed a good understanding of how cells work, they have discovered that cells can be manipulated to create food, conquer disease, and form biofuel.

The practical applications of what can be learned and done with cell science appear to be endless and have led to new fields. These include biotechnology, bioengineering, and biomedicine.

Cells: Experience Life at Its Tiniest will introduce you to the vast and exciting field of cell science. You will understand the functions and processes of cells in various living organisms. You will learn how scientists are using cell science to treat diseases and injuries. You will also learn how cell science is solving many of the world's problems. Perhaps you will use cell science one day to make a difference in the world.

KEY QUESTIONS

- How did people explain life before the discovery of cells?
- How did the invention of the microscope contribute to the study of biology?
- How does "cell theory" help us understand living things?

SAFETY

Safety in the science classroom, laboratory, or field site is the first priority. The following safety rules and procedures are adopted from the National Science Teachers Association.

- Conduct yourself responsibly at all times. A science lab or station is not a place for play.

- Read all safety information ahead of time.

- No eating or drinking around experiments. Do not touch your face.

- Work in a lab or science station should always be supervised by an adult.

- Wear safety goggles as needed and lab gloves with any activities that require touching cells.

- Clean up all spills.

- Wear appropriate clothing, remove jewelry, and tie hair back.

Know the location of safety equipment, including eye wash stations and fire extinguishers.

- lenses from disposable cameras (remove battery first, then use insulated tools with the help of an experienced adult) or purchased lenses
- plastic tubes slightly wider in diameter than the lenses
- black opaque paper
- metal and plastic washers
- small light source
- 35 mm film canister or something similar in size
- glue gun

BUILD A MICROSCOPE

Microscopes have come a long way since the Dutch first created compound and simple microscopes. A microscope is simply an optical device that magnifies objects. Many standard microscopes have built-in light sources to improve the view. We call them compound light microscopes. These compound microscopes have a lens in the eyepiece and more lenses closer to the specimen.

- You can learn about different microscopes available to purchase at this website.

 homeschool scientists microscope

- Interested in using a smart phone or computer to magnify objects? Get more information here.

 Wired cellphone microscope

What type of microscope will work best for you in exploring cell science? Is it something you buy, download, or perhaps make yourself?

1. Eyepiece
2. Revolving nose piece (holds objective lenses)
3. Objective lens
4. Focus knob for coarse adjustment
5. Focus knob for fine adjustment
6. Stage or platform (holds the slides/specimens)
7. Light source
8. Diaphragm and condenser focuses the quality and intensity of light
9. Mechanical stage, optional part found on higher-end microscopes to adjust slide

- **Research building microscopes on the Internet.** You may find blueprints to download or perhaps discover another idea for how to create one. Don't be afraid to be creative when figuring out a design for a microscope. Engineers learn about their own products by making mistakes and improving their own designs. Draw your design ideas in your science journal.

- **Once you have some ideas, try building your favorite design.** Test it out by looking at a variety of specimens. Can you use it to magnify samples for studying them?

- **Figure out how to make your design even better and build another microscope.** Will you use more lenses? Larger lenses? Maybe you'll find a different light source. Remember, people are still improving the functions of the microscopes scientists use in professional labs. There is always a better microscope to build.

To investigate more, research Stanford engineer Manu Prakash, who created a paper microscope called a foldscope that could withstand the hazards of the Amazon region in South America. He talks about the benefits of easily accessible, inexpensive microscopes here.

Does he inspire you to try some new ideas?

🔍 Stanford Medicine foldscope

SCIENTIFIC METHOD

Keep a science journal to record your methods and observations during all the activities in this book. You can use a scientific method worksheet to keep your ideas and observations organized.

Question: What are we trying to find out? What problem are we trying to solve?

Research: What do other people think?

Hypothesis: What do we think the answer will be?

Equipment: What supplies are we using?

Method: What procedure are we following?

Results: What happened and why?

SPONTANEOUS GENERATION

In 1859, Louis Pasteur disproved spontaneous generation in his famous beaker experiment. Any scientific experiment must be validated, which means to do the same experiment again and again to make certain the results are the same. Can you do a version of Pasteur's experiment?

- **Begin a scientific method worksheet and come up with your supplies, experiment steps, and hypothesis.**

  - How will you set up two groups to test your hypothesis?

  - How can you ensure that you are only testing one aspect about your substances?

- **Can you think of any improvements to make to the experiment?** Perform your experiment and record your observations.

  - How long does it take to see change?

  - What happens to each substance?

  - What happens when you make changes to the substances and alter the environment?

To investigate more, alter another aspect of the substance and test to see if this makes a difference in your results. Do you think there would be differences in outcomes if you factored sunlight and darkness into this experiment? What would your hypothesis be? What are your results?

Chapter 1 ▶

How Do Cells Work?

JUST LIKE HUMANS, CELLS HAVE DIFFERENT PARTS!

What are the parts of a cell and what do they do?

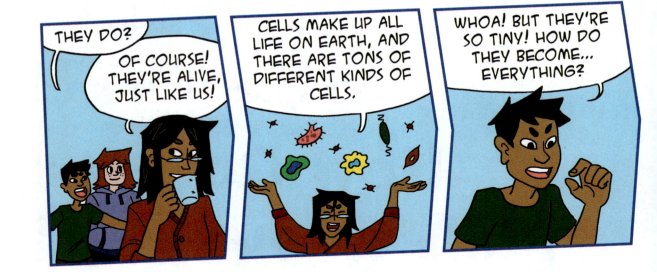

Cells have different components that perform different functions. These functions allow the cell to be a thriving part of a living organism.

Science writer Adam Rutherford describes a cell as "a hive of densely packed activity receiving input from its environment." Cells stay busy 24 hours a day, seven days a week, building, growing, repairing, communicating, and reproducing. Most cells are too small to be seen with the naked eye. While they might be microscopic in size, they make all life possible.

Every cell and every structure within a cell has specific functions. To understand the role of cells in our own lives and in life around us, it is important to learn about a cell's structure and how it works.

TYPES OF CELLS

Organisms can be either unicellular or multicellular. Unicellular organisms have just a single cell. These single-cell organisms are the bacteria, archaea, and some fungi.

All living things can be categorized into one of three groups, called domains. Two of the three domains include the single-celled organisms bacteria and archaea. The third domain contains more complex organisms called eukaryotes. This is the domain that includes humans.

Each of the many cells within a multicellular organism has a function. Each cell communicates with other cells to fulfill its role.

In 1833, Scottish scientist Robert Brown (1773–1858) noticed tiny cloudy spots in the centers of cells. Each looked like a seed, so he called it a nucleus, which is Latin for "kernel of a nut." Brown didn't know exactly what the nucleus did, but he suspected it was very important. And he was right.

Cells that contain a nucleus are called eukaryotes. The Greek origin of *karyon* means "nut, kernel, or seed." The word *eu* means "good." *Eukaryote* is "good seed." The genetic material of eukaryotic cells, or the DNA, is contained in the nucleus. This material dictates what the cell does.

Most eukaryote organisms are multicellular, such as plants and animals. However, some unicellular fungi and microscopic organisms, known as protists, are eukaryotic, too.

Cells without a nucleus are called prokaryotes. *Pro* means "before," and *prokaryote* means "before seed." Prokaryotes are unicellular organisms, including bacteria, archaea, and cyanobacteria, which is also known as blue-green algae.

When we think of bacteria, we often think of what makes us sick. But there are beneficial bacteria as well that keep us healthy!

Multi-celled organisms known as eukaryotes have been around for only about 600 million years. For most of our planet's history, the organisms were unicellular.

There is another difference between prokaryotic and eukaryotic cells. Eukaryotes have organelles, or little organs. Each organelle carries out a specific task in the cell, much like your own organs carry out specific tasks in your body. One of your organs is your stomach. Its function is to digest food. Another organ is the heart, which pumps blood to every part of your body, delivering oxygen and nutrients that keep you healthy and alive. Just as your organs have certain functions, so do the organelles of eukaryotic cells.

Scientists puzzled over organelles in cells for a long time. How did these structures, these little organs, get inside the cells in the first place?

Scientists believe that about 600 million years ago, single cells became part of larger cells. One prokaryote "swallowed" another and the cells formed symbiotic relationships. This means they were beneficial to each other.

SEEING THE CELL'S STRUCTURE

As technology advanced, new tools led to new discoveries. Microscopes have been through significant changes during the 400 years that they've been around.

Standard microscopes, called light microscopes, are what you are probably most familiar with. They can magnify an object's size hundreds of times. Today, there are also electron microscopes that magnify objects millions of times. Instead of light, electron microscopes use electrons to enhance the view of an object. Electron microscopes are expensive to buy and maintain and can usually be found only in science laboratories and universities.

In the 1860s and 1870s, scientists learned that they could stain cell samples in order to better see the cell structure under a microscope. Different stains bring out specific components and details. Another device, the ultra centrifuge, spins substances at such high speeds that a cell separates, leaving heavier parts to sink and the lightest to rise to the top. This technique allows scientists to separate parts of a cell, such as the nucleus and other organelles. These tools have helped us learn much about cells.

> Whether a cell is a eukaryote
> or a prokaryote, all cells
> share some similarities.

One similarity is that they all have an outer layer. Just as your skin is an outer layer that covers your body and protects it from the environment, a cell has a cell membrane that covers and protects it.

Proteins make up almost half of the cell membrane. The membrane is also made of carbohydrates, phospholipids, and sterols, which are called cholesterol in animals. The membrane is a fluid, flexible barrier, and very picky about what it allows to pass through. It lets in certain food molecules to feed the cell. This food is converted into energy that makes it possible for cells to function.

LYNN MARGULIS AND THE ENDOSYMBIOTIC THEORY

In the 1960s, an American biologist named Lynn Margulis (1938–2011) first proposed the endosymbiotic theory. This is the idea that eukaryotic organisms evolved through symbiotic relationships between cells. Seeing many similarities between organelles and single-cell bacteria, she hypothesized that these organelles evolved from single-cell organisms. Margulis published the theory in 1971 in *The Origin of Eukaryotic Cells*, but received great criticism from the scientific world for her ideas. As research advanced, she was proven right. She finally received recognition for her contributions, including the 1999 National Medal of Science from President Bill Clinton. You can read an interview with her at this website.

Discover Magazine Lynn Margulis

All cells are also filled with fluid called cytoplasm. Cytoplasm contains many nutrients that support the activity within cells. Molecules travel around the cell's cytoplasm.

All cells contain DNA, or deoxyribonucleic acid. DNA holds the blueprints of a cell, or information on how that cell develops and functions. This genetic material is housed in the nucleus of eukaryotes. In prokaryotes, there is no well-defined nucleus. Instead, genetic material is made up of a single DNA molecule that lives in a specific region of the cell, called the nucleoid.

Proteins are a very important part of a cell. They are similar to the worker ants of an ant colony, which make sure everything gets done to ensure survival. Some proteins help with transportation, while others drive the cell function.

Cells have to manufacture these proteins, and they do this with ribosomes from ribosomal RNA (rRNA). Although both eukaryotes and prokaryotes have ribosomes, the ribosomes in prokaryotes are smaller than those in eukaryotes.

CELL FUNCTION

Cells have a variety of functions. In unicellular organisms, the single cell is responsible for everything. Prokaryotes have a high growth rate. Much of their focus is on growing and dividing.

Multicellular organisms are like large factories, with different cells having different functions. Some cells make food, while others make repairs. Each cell has a specific job to do. For example, some cells attach to each other to form tissue within an organism. These tissues also have particular functions, such as heart tissue or liver tissue.

Within a cell, all parts have their own roles to play to make the cell operate smoothly and contribute to the health and well-being of the organism as a whole. The nucleus is like the command center of a cell. Its function is to store and protect the DNA with its own membrane, called the nuclear membrane, or envelope.

Like the cell membrane, the nuclear envelope is selective about what it lets in and out. One of the things it allows through are nucleotides. These molecules are used by the nucleus to build DNA and RNA molecules. RNA molecules and the ribosomes exit the nuclear membrane to the cytoplasm.

Many organelles also have their own membranes. A mitochondrion is an important rod-shaped organelle that functions as a cell's power plant. Mitochondria have two membranes to help convert food into energy that the cell can use in a process known as cellular respiration. The energy molecule that results from cellular respiration is called adenosine triphosphate, or ATP.

[
The next time you take a run or a bike ride, you can thank ATP for giving your muscle cells the energy they need to be active.
]

Communication is very important between cells. Just as families work better when the members communicate, so do the cells in a multicellular organism. They use cell signaling to communicate both between cells that are very close to each other and between cells that are far apart. Chemical signals can be carried by molecules or mechanical signals can come from forces upon a cell and within a cell.

When we talk about proteins in cells, we are talking about chains of amino acids. There are 20 types of amino acids that make up proteins. Proteins are some of the most complex molecules, each with a unique sequence of amino acids. There are about 20,000 distinct proteins in humans. Most cells in the human body contain about 10 billion protein molecules in each cell.

A TOUR OF A CELL

Take a tour of the cell at the National Science Foundation.

🔍 NSF tour of the cell

Refer back to this diagram of a eukaryotic cell as you read through the rest of the book and discover what role each organelle plays.

We've been talking about the little organs or organelles of eukaryotic cells, but all cells contain these similar structures.

- Cell or plasma membrane, the outer covering that protects the cell.

- Cytoplasm, the jelly-like substance in the cell that provides nutrients and also holds structures more or less in place.

- DNA, the genetic material used for the cell to reproduce.

- Ribosomes, the protein-making machine of the cell.

In addition, all cells need energy to function and survive. They get this energy from carbohydrates, fats, and proteins.

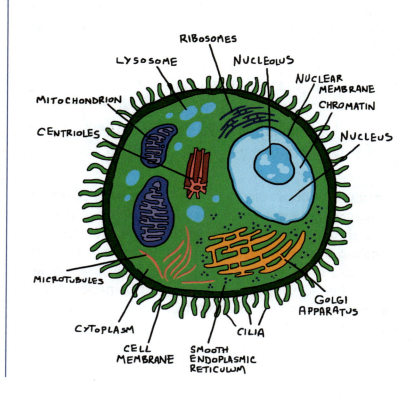

MOVEMENT WITHIN THE CELL

In the early nineteenth century, French physiologist Henri Dutrochi (1776–1847) observed materials moving in and out of cells through the membrane. He called this method of transportation osmosis. Some molecules move across the membrane freely, while others need help from protein transporters.

Molecules move within the cell, too, where it can get crowded. They move from areas where there is a high concentration of molecules to an area where there are fewer molecules. Known as diffusion, this helps molecules stay equally distributed in a cell.

Active transport within a cell uses ATP to help move molecules. They move through the cytoplasm and into the nucleus, too.

Another important movement that takes place in cells involves messenger RNA (mRNA). Ribonucleic acid is a molecule made from DNA. When certain proteins are needed in the cell, the genetic information for that protein is copied from DNA to RNA. This process is called transcription. Then mRNA carries the code to the ribosomes to produce the needed proteins.

AMOEBA DANCE

Although all cells have some capacity to move at some stages, cells differ in how active they are and in how they move. Check out this Amoeba proteus moving.

PS

Exploratorium cell motility

CELLS HELP EACH OTHER OUT, TOO. IF THERE'S AN IMBALANCE OF MOLECULES, THEY CAN USE *DIFFUSION* TO BALANCE IT ALL OUT!

WOW, WHO KNEW I WOULD LEARN SO MUCH FROM MOLDY CHEESE!

Whole cells can move as well. The cytoskeleton, the structure that connects to every part of the cell membrane, of some cells can break down and reform, allowing cells to crawl along. Some cells have cilia surrounding the outside of the cell. When seen under a microscope, cilia resemble eyelashes that go all around the cell. Cilia help a cell perform a swimming movement. Other cells might have a flagella, which is more like a tail. There are fewer flagella, but they're longer than the cilia. They work like the kick of a swim stroke to push the cell along.

CELL DIVISION

In the early 1850s, Belgian botanist Barthélemy Dumortier (1797–1878) observed plant cells doing a curious thing under his microscope. The cells split in half and became two new cells. About the same time, physiologist Robert Remak (1815–1865) reported seeing something similar happening with animal cells.

Cells divide for three reasons: growth, repair, and reproduction. A tree that starts as a sapling and grows to its full size has cells dividing for growth. The cells that make up your skin are always dividing to make new skin and to repair any skin that gets damaged. Living organisms also reproduce through cell division.

Prokaryotic organisms, such as bacteria, divide through a process called binary fission. Here's how it works. The cell makes a copy of its chromosome. The bacteria cell continues to grow, making copies of other things it needs, such as ribosomes. Then, an equal number of cell molecules moves to each side of a cell, and the one cell splits in half to become two cells.

Single-cell eukaryotes divide quickly when food is available, but with multicellular eukaryotes, cell division is more complicated. Cells divide at different rates in multicellular organisms.

As we mentioned earlier, cells that make up skin are always dividing. They're also constantly dividing in the mucous membranes, such as in your nose, as dead cells are shed from the body.

Other cells divide only when they receive a signal that damage has occurred. For example, a chemical signal is emitted when there is damage to any of our organs. When they receive this signal, cells begin to divide to replace the damaged cells.

When a cell is not dividing, it is often growing. This is called the interphase and is where cells spend the majority of their time.

[The entire process of growth and division is called the cell cycle. Animal cell cycles typically last from 8 to 24 hours.]

The interphase part of the cell cycle has three subphases. Cells spend a lot of time in the first subphase, called Gap 1 (G1). During this time, the cell copies all of its contents except for DNA. Before the cell moves into the second subphase, called the Synthesis, or S phase, it must pass through the checkpoint.

The checkpoint is like an exam. Think of it as the process you must go through before you first get your driver's license. You have to pass driver's education, correct your vision to 20/20, have insurance, and pass a driver's test. Each of these things must be checked off before you receive your license.

In order for a cell to pass from the G1 to the S phase, the cell must receive a signal to divide and be large enough to divide. It must contain plenty of nutrients and have DNA in good condition. If a cell doesn't meet these conditions, repairs are made. If a cell can't pass even after repairs, it will cease to function and die.

A PIONEER OF CELL DIVISION

Ernest Everett Just (1883–1941) attended college when few African Americans were admitted. He was the only person in his class at Dartmouth College to graduate magna cum laude (with honors). He received his PhD in experimental embryology from the University of Chicago, and was interested in cell division, the effect of ultraviolet rays in increasing numbers of chromosomes in animals, and the effects of dehydration on living cells.

The cells of the nervous system can't be repaired like other cells. That's why injuries to the spine often lead to permanent damage or paralysis.

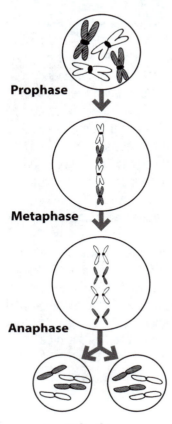

MITOSIS

Prophase

Metaphase

Anaphase

Telophase

The mitotic spindle is a group of cytoskeletal proteins called microtubules that separate the two copies of chromosomes from one parent cell into two daughter cells during mitosis.

Cells that pass to the S phase copy their DNA and then proceed to the last subphase, Gap 2, where the work is checked again. This checkpoint requires certain conditions before cell division, called mitosis. All chromosomes have to be copied and the DNA must be in good condition and free of damage. Once a signal to proceed to mitosis has been received, division begins.

MITOSIS

There are two processes of cell division for multicellular organisms: mitosis and meiosis. Most cells in your body use mitosis to divide. Mitosis is more common than meiosis. All living organisms use mitosis. During mitosis, identical cells are reproduced to replace injured or old cells. They contain the same chromosomes as the parent cells.

Mitosis has four phases for cell division. In the first phase, called prophase, the nuclear membrane breaks down and allows the mitotic spindle to attach to the chromosomes, which are now visible as they coil and condense. In the second phase, called metaphase, the chromosomes are lined up and attached to the middle of the mitotic spindle.

Once the chromosomes are organized, the cell enters the third phase, called anaphase. The chromosome copies, called chromatids, separate. One part of an identical pair goes to one side of the cell, and the other chromatid goes to the opposite side. The actual splitting of the cell into two daughter cells, called cytokinesis, occurs in this last phase.

During telophase, the two sides of the cell separate and the nuclear membrane reforms. Chromosomes uncoil and become invisible. Where there was once one cell, there are now two cells.

MEIOSIS

Meiosis is the cell division that occurs in special cells in sexually reproducing organisms. Meiosis produces egg cells and sperm cells that have half of the genetic makeup of an individual, since they will eventually combine to form an embryo. During meiosis, a parent cell goes through two complete rounds of division. In the first round, called Meiosis I, two daughter cells are produced. In Meiosis II, the two daughter cells divide to produce four granddaughter cells, called gametes. Each gamete has half of the chromosomes of the parent cell.

Gametes become the sex cells, either egg cells in women or sperm cells in men. When an egg cell is fertilized by a sperm cell, the new cell is called a zygote. Since the zygote contains half the chromosomes from the egg cell and half from the sperm cell, it is a genetically unique cell.

Although at first glance through a microscope, a cell doesn't look like much, it's really a highly tuned component of life. Cells have many similarities, but may have different functions and purposes. To understand the evolution of cells, it's important to start at the beginning, with single-cell life.

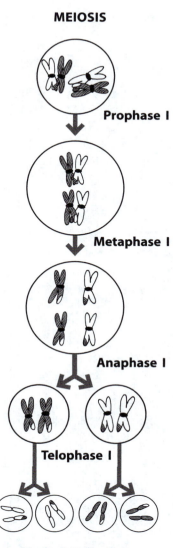

MEIOSIS

Prophase I

Metaphase I

Anaphase I

Telophase I

End of Meiosis II

KEY QUESTIONS

- **What are the two types of cells? What is the chief difference between them?**
- **How do you explain the relationship between the structures and functions of cell organelles?**
- **Why is each part of the cell essential to survival?**
- **How is a living organism the sum of all of its parts?**

VOCAB LAB

Write down what you think each word means. What root words can you find for help?

binary fission, centrifuge, eukaryote, meiosis, mitochondria, mitosis, nucleotide, organelle, osmosis, prokaryote, and **symbiotic**.

Compare your definitions with those of your friends or classmates. Did you all come up with the same meanings? Turn to the text and glossary if you need help.

EUKARYOTIC CELL MODEL

A eukaryotic cell is a complicated cell with lots of components. To better understand its parts and how they function, create a three-dimensional model of this kind of cell.

- **With an adult's permission, research cell structure diagrams on the Internet.** Find one you would like to make a model of.

- **Decide on the materials you will use to create your model.**

  - How will you distinguish between the organelles?

  - What can you use for cytoplasm?

  - How can you provide a key so that observers will know what you're looking at and what the function is of each structure?

To investigate more, find another cell to model and use different materials. How about making an edible model? What sort of supplies can you use to create a cell model you can eat?

Chapter 2 ▶

Discovering Single-Cell Life

What are the different species of single-cell organisms and how do they behave?

There are many different kinds of single-cell organisms. They share many similarities, but also have plenty of differences.

Before dinosaurs walked the earth, long before plants and animals existed, there were bacteria and archaea, single-cell organisms that made it possible for all life that followed.

It's believed the earth was formed about 4.6 billion years ago and the first cells emerged about 750 million years after that. How life came to be is the stuff of theories. Remember how theories are proven using the scientific method? Well, cell scientists haven't been able to reproduce the beginning of life in a laboratory.

About 4 billion years ago, our planet was very different from what it is today. Gases and oceans that reached the boiling point made up the earth. A popular theory is that in these high-energy conditions, organic molecules formed that grew larger and more complex. The building blocks of life formed—nucleic acids, proteins, sugars, and fats that have carbon and hydrogen as their backbone.

Eventually, tiny, single-cell organisms developed. These microbes are the oldest form of life on earth. They're the single-cell creatures you can't see—bacteria, archaea, protists, and some fungi. Each ranges in size from 1 micron (one-millionth of a meter) to 100 microns. A micron is an abbreviation for micrometer. A single hair from your head is only about 40 to 50 microns wide.

We exist because of these microbes. And we will continue to thrive because of them. Microbes can exist without us, but we can't exist without microbes. They make it possible for us to digest food and stay healthy. Without them, we couldn't even breathe.

[Microbes are so tiny that it would take millions to fill the eye of a needle.]

There are microbes all over and inside your body! Everything we touch has microbes and those microbes like nothing better than finding a new home . . . including your hands. Millions of microbes live on your hands, and while most are beneficial or harmless, some can make you sick.

Let's take a look at the different kinds of microbes.

BACTERIA

Bacteria, members of the Monera kingdom, are the most abundant form of life in the world. Go outside and get a handful of soil and you'll likely be holding at least 1 billion bacteria. Your body contains 10 times more bacteria cells than human cells!

TAXONOMY

Taxonomy is the science of classifying organisms, in which they are named and described. Relationships with other organisms become part of the classification as families of organisms are created.

The naming and classifying of organisms is an ongoing process. Fewer than 2 million species of organisms have been classified. It's estimated that this may only be 13 percent of all species. To view the taxonomy of a specific organism, you can visit this website.

🔍 Integrated Taxonomic Information System

Classification system of all living things:

LIFE
DOMAIN
KINGDOM
PHYLUM
CLASS
ORDER
FAMILY
GENUS
SPECIES

For about 1 billion years, bacteria were the only form of life. Living in shallow waters, these bacteria performed the important function of creating atmospheric oxygen. Oxygen in the air made it possible for more complex, multicellular organisms to develop.

Even single-cell organisms can communicate. Bacteria use chemical signals to discover how many other bacteria are in the area, while yeast use chemical signals to find mates.

Look at bacteria under a microscope, and you'll probably see one or more of the three most common shapes of bacteria—bacilli, cocci, and spirilla. The rod-shaped bacteria are called bacilli. Cocci are the sphere-shaped bacteria. The third type, spirilla, are spiral-shaped. There are also less common shapes, such as comma bacteria, virios and corkscrew-shaped bacteria, and spirochaetes.

Bacteria can also be classified by how they respond to oxygen. Aerobic bacteria need oxygen to live and thrive. Other bacteria, such as the bacteria that live on the ocean floor, are anaerobic. This means they do not require oxygen to live. There are also bacteria that prefer oxygen but can grow without it.

Like people, bacteria might live alone or in pairs or in a group. However, bacteria are hardier than us. They live on land, in water, in heat and cold. They can absorb sunlight, iron, sulfur, and more. But the favorite "food" for most bacteria are sugars and starches.

These microbes do plenty of good things, such as turn milk into yogurt and cheese and make them taste so good. Some antibiotics that help us fight infections are made from bacteria. A very beneficial type of bacteria is cyanobacteria. Like plants, cyanobacteria use photosynthesis to convert sunlight into energy and oxygen. Cyanobacteria live in the water and are sometimes referred to as blue-green algae.

The types of bacteria that lead to disease and infection are actually a small percentage of bacteria. But they can make you sick, from intestinal problems to ear infections. If you've ever had strep throat, you know the bad side of bacteria. This common illness is caused by streptococcal bacteria, which cause inflammation and swelling of the mucous membranes in the back of the throat.

Other dangerous bacteria include bacillus anthracis, which causes anthrax. This disease kills cows. Some humans have even used it as a weapon. When we hear about E. coli (Escherichia coli), we think about food poisoning, but there are good E. coli in your gut right now that are digesting food and producing vitamin K.

Bacteria are the simplest of organisms, with a single loop of DNA. They have no nuclei and no organelles. Surrounding the plasma membrane is a cell wall.

Various kinds of bacteria move around differently. Some use flagella to swim around. Others glide around with a thick, slimy layer called a capsule. Some use spikes to grip surfaces.

Remember, all cells need energy! Bacteria obtain energy in one of two ways. Both ways are beneficial to the environment and, together, help maintain the balance of carbon and oxygen in the environment. Those that break down organic materials in the environment are called heterotrophs. As the bacteria break down materials such as rotting leaves and even dead bodies, the carbon within the material is released into the environment.

Autotrophs are bacteria that make their own food from carbon dioxide, along with light energy or oxidized elements. Cyanobacteria are an example of this type.

ARCHAEA

Archaea look a lot like bacteria. Under a microscope, you might see these rod- or sphere-shaped organisms living among bacteria. Many archaea move like bacteria, using flagella.

But there are differences. Archaea cell walls are made up of different types of amino acids and sugars. Some archaea have cell walls, while others don't.

BACTERIA FOSSILS

The oldest fossils discovered are of cyanobacteria from approximately 3 billion years ago. In the late 1960s, scientists discovered cyanobacteria fossils near South Africa. In 1980, more fossils were found in rock at the North Pole. Cyanobacteria are among the largest forms of bacteria and contain thick cell walls, which may explain why they are capable of leaving behind fossils. You can see the fossil here.

PS

Berkeley cyanobacteria

The cell membranes of archaea also differ from bacterial cell membranes in structure and composition.

> Antibiotics, which slow or kill certain kinds of bacteria and which might be prescribed to you if you're sick, have no effect on archaea.

Archaea were discovered and given a name quite recently, only in the 1970s! At the time, scientists decided archaea were truly another life form that deserved its own taxonomy. Their name comes from the Greek, meaning "ancient." Archaea, described as living fossils, are useful for scientists studying evolution.

Scientists believe that bacteria and archaea had a common ancestor before splitting into two different type of organisms. Millions of years after that, archaea split again. Some continued as single-cell prokaryotes. Others evolved into eukaryotic organisms, leading to the creation of plants, animals, and you!

EXTREME ARCHAEA

Archaea feed on hydrogen gas, carbon dioxide, and sulfur. Many archaea are extreme organisms that like living in extreme environments where few other organisms could survive. These include boiling waters, such as those found in geysers and hydrothermal vents, or the frigid cold found under Arctic ice.

Some enjoy acidic environments, such as those in certain lakes or in volcanoes with an extremely high sulfur content. Others like life salty, living in locations such as the Great Salt Lake or the Dead Sea, where a lot of salt is present. Many salt-loving archaea produce methane gas.

PROTISTS

The protists are interesting organisms. They can be plant-like and make their own food through photosynthesis. They can also be animal-like and feed on other organisms and reproduce with partners, just as multicellular organisms do. Protists use flagella, cilia, or cell extensions to move.

Protists are eukaryotic single-cell organisms, unlike bacteria and archaea, which are prokaryotic. This means protists have a nucleus and share other similarities to many different types of organisms, including fungi, plants, and animals. In fact, scientists believe protists may have played a part in the development of these multicellular organisms.

There are four main types of protists—algae, protozoa, slime molds, and water molds. Algae behave like many plants. Most algae are single-cell, but there are some multicellular forms of algae. Seaweed is a type of multicellular algae.

Single-cell algae live on or near water and are an important part of the food chain. Phytoplankton is an example of single-cell algae. Species that live near the surface of the water might depend on sunlight for photosynthesis, just as plants do. Green algae, with its high levels of chlorophyll, might have been a precursor to plants. You'll learn in the next chapter how plants use chlorophyll in the process of photosynthesis. If you've ever seen a layer of green scum on water, this is likely green algae.

The word *protozoa* means "first animals." This single-cell organism lives in soil and water around the world. It is both a hunter and grazer when it comes to food. Protozoa often feed on other microbes. They maintain balance in the microbe world and are another important part of the food chain.

In 2015, the Virginia Tech Department of Biomedical Engineering and Mechanics performed a study showing that single-cell organisms can move in many different ways, including somersaults. Students observed how protozoans called paramecium moved according to obstacles in their habitat, even if that meant some acrobatic moves.

Some protozoa species are dangerous, however. Plasmodium vivax is a parasite that lives in mosquitoes until it finds a human host. Once it enters a human, it causes a disease called malaria.

Slime mold is a land-based mold that seems similar to fungi. It can and does appear everywhere, but a popular location is on forest floors, where it breaks down rotting vegetation. A common type of slime mold are amoeba, which have multiple nuclei.

Imagine going into your backyard to find a large, jelly-like mass about 14 inches in diameter pulsating in the yard! Someone in Dallas, Texas, found exactly that in the 1970s. Scientists determined that it wasn't an alien life form, just a larger-than-normal slime mold.

There are more than 900 species of slime mold, which come in all shapes and colors (except green, since it doesn't contain chlorophyll). Some even look like honeycombs. Most are microscopic, but others can grow as long as 10 to 13 feet. Slime mold often moves toward prey, then surrounds and consumes it. It eats bacteria and fungus. If food is limited, several organisms will form into a mass to work together.

The fourth type of protist is water mold, technically known as oomycota. The word *oomycota* means "egg fungi," which fits because of the round shapes of water mold. Water mold was once thought to be fungi because, like fungi, it also has branching, threadlike structures called filaments and feeds on decaying tissue. Yet the cell wall and nucleus of water molds are different from those of fungi.

Water mold needs a wet environment, where it breaks down and recycles decaying organisms. There are more than 500 species of water mold—some of these are parasitic and destroy animals and plants. Some species grow on fish or amphibians. More, however, attack flowering plants.

> In the mid-1800s, a water mold called Phytophthora infestans destroyed potato plants in Europe.

The spread of the water mold led to the Great Potato Famine in Ireland, resulting in the death of almost a million people.

SINGLE-CELL LIFE CYCLE

Single-cell organisms can be prokaryotes or eukaryotes. Most prokaryotes divide by binary fission. Reproduction can be rapid when conditions are right. Here's how it happens.

The DNA within the cell is replicated so there are two sets of chromosomes. As the cell divides through mitosis, a process described on page 24, each set of chromosomes becomes part of a new cell.

Other single-cell organisms can reproduce only with the help of their hosts. This is true for the bacteria in your body that help you digest your food, also known as flora. The host (in this case, you) provides nutrients and the right type of environment to help these bacteria complete their life cycle. Some single-cell organisms even make use of their host DNA to help with replication.

Protists and fungi (including yeast), are single-cell eukaryotes. Amoebas are an often-studied protist. Like bacteria, these cells reproduce by binary fission. Have you ever observed an amoeba under a microscope? It looks as though the amoeba simply splits in half to form two new amoebas.

COOL CONCEPT

Who says you need a brain to learn? In 2016, scientists at a French university reported on experiments with protists in which they placed a food source on the other side of harmless but bitter substances. The protists seemed to learn that the substances were harmless, then crossed them rapidly in order to reach the food.

AMOEBA MAZE

Slime molds spread like highway networks. Experiments with this soil-dwelling protist show that it is able to figure out how to cover the most area while using the least amount of energy. They can even solve mazes! You can watch this feat at this website.

🔍 amoeba solve maze video

PS

Many single-cell organisms feed on smaller single-cell organisms. They are all parts of the food chain. Protists feed on bacteria, while fish and insects feed on protists.

HUMONGOUS FUNGUS

Some fungi, such as the honey mushroom, or Armillaria solidipes, can grow to extremely large sizes. The largest recorded is the one in Oregon's Malheur National Forest, which covers 2,200 acres. You can see this impressive creature here.

fungus Oregon Malheur National Forest

Amoebas have pseudopods that help them move and eat. An amoeba can stretch out the pseudopod and pull the rest of its body along in a crawling motion. It can also use the pseudopod to surround food and bring it back. Amoebas eat dead plant and animal matter, as well as bacteria, algae, and other protozoa.

FUNGUS STRADDLES BOTH WORLDS

Have you ever seen mushrooms growing? You might think they were plants. Scientists once believed fungi belonged in the plant kingdom. But when they were able to look at the DNA of fungi, they realized mushrooms aren't plants.

For one thing, fungi do not make their own food as plants do. Fungi feed on organic matter, absorbing sugars through their cell walls. Like some bacteria, fungi release an enzyme that turns dead organisms into a sort of molecule soup that they can absorb as energy, Fungi are often called the earth's scavengers because they feed on dead plants and animals.

Fungi cells are different from plant cells in other ways, too. In plants, each cell is separated from the others by a cell wall. In fungi cells, the cell walls have openings that allow nuclei, proteins, and fluid to flow from one cell to another. In some species, there are no walls dividing cells. Instead, there is just a long cell with multiple nuclei.

Is fungi single-cell or multicellular? The answer is both! Yeast and some molds are examples of single-cell fungi, but most fungi are multicellular. Whether yeast, mold, or mushroom, they all have a nucleus that houses their DNA, so they are eukaryotic.

Many multicellular fungi are visible. Fungi that feed on trees might not be visible at first, but will be as they grow larger. The most common multicellular fungus is the mushroom. Some varieties of mushrooms are food sources while others are deadly.

Fungi don't move or grow like other organisms. Instead, they spread through reproductive spores carried by wind and rain or by extended threads of cells called hyphae. Hyphae continue growing by adding cells at the tip. These are very tiny cells, but can push through animal cells and plant cells.

Like bacteria, fungi can be beneficial or detrimental to humans. Beneficial fungi include the yeast that makes bread rise and edible mushrooms. But when fungus grows on old food, it can make you sick. Other species, such as Candida, are poisonous. Some fungi can also attach themselves to crops and destroy them.

Single-cell organisms are the oldest form of life on the planet, and they continue to be necessary for all life to continue. It was single-cell life that gave birth to the first multicellular organisms—plants. We'll read more about plants in the next chapter.

KEY QUESTIONS

- **What is the difference between prokaryotic and eukaryotic single-cell organisms? How are they similar?**
- **How are single-cell organisms beneficial to the human world? In what ways can they hurt us?**
- **How do most bacteria reproduce?**
- **Why are fungi in a separate taxonomy group from plants?**

MICROBIAL MERGERS

Another class of single-cell organisms are microbial mergers. An example are the microbes in our digestive system. Humans and these microbes have developed important, symbiotic relationships in which both organisms benefit from each other. Other examples of microbial mergers are rhizobia. These bacteria attach to the roots of legumes to provide them with nitrogen. Then the legumes supply rhizobia with carbohydrates for food. Zooxanthellae are algae that live in the tissues of coral. The coral gets nutrients and the algae receives an environment that will allow it to thrive. Algae that join with fungi form lichens. Lichens are a microbial merger. By joining, the fungi and algae allows each to grow in environments they couldn't normally survive in alone, such as tree bark or rocks.

VOCAB LAB

Write down what you think each word means. What root words can you find for help?

aerobic, amoeba, anaerobic, archaea, autotroph, bacilli, cilia, cocci, cyanobacteria, flagella, fungus, heterotroph, microbe, protists, protozoa, and **spirilla.**

Compare your definitions with those of your friends or classmates. Did you all come up with the same meanings? Turn to the text and glossary if you need help.

USING A MICROSCOPE

Using a microscope, you can see microbes for yourself. Prepared slides can be purchased from supply companies, but look around and you might find other samples. Yogurt has bacteria. Bacteria can sometimes be scraped off of certain types of cheese, such as Limburger. Dirt from your backyard and water from the neighborhood pond or creek are also possibilities.

- Use this simulation tool from the University of Delaware to help prepare to use microscopes.

microscope simulator

Using a microscope involves more than simply focusing. You must also prepare the slide. Slides are rectangular pieces of glass or plastic that measure about 1 by 3 inches. The cover slip helps with specimen viewing and protects the microscope lens from getting wet. Slides and cover slips can be reused after cleaning.

Preparing a slide is called a slide mount. A wet mount is most common. Using a dropper, place a drop of a wet sample on a slide, then gently lay a cover slip over it without applying pressure. Place the slide on the microscope stage. Wet mounts usually only last about 15 to 30 minutes before drying up.

One trick to make slide mounts last longer is to place a little petroleum jelly on the corners of the cover slip. Then lay it on the slide, petroleum jelly–side down. This creates a seal that may preserve the slide up to a few days.

Dry mounts use no water. They are used mostly with cells that are already dead. A cover slip holds the specimen in place.

Search on the Internet for "Science Supply Companies" for items such as slides, cover slips, and other items needed for use with a microscope. Supply companies also sell chemicals and stains. One chemical, called a quieting solution, slows down protozoa so they can be better observed. Stains are used to better view different parts of a cell structure. Vital stains work on live cells, and non-vital stains can work on dead cells or tissue. You can also purchase pre-stained samples.

Caution: Gloves should always be worn to protect yourself and your samples from contamination.

- **Prepare slides with different substances to use with your microscope.** Place one on the microscope stage and attach it. Hold slides only by their edges.

- **Turn the focus knob so that the stage moves closer to the objective lens without touching.** Look through the eyepiece. Use the focus knob to get a clear view.

- **Describe what you see in your science journal.** You can also use sketches to record your observations. Label your notes. Can you identify the bacteria you see?

- **When you are finished with the slide, lower the stage and then remove the slide.** Examine your other slides in a similar way.

SUPPLIES

Try these online resources for supplies!

Fisher Science Education

Carolina

To investigate more, try using other objects from nature and other foods. What similarities do you see? Do all objects that you sample under your microscope show bacteria? If not, why do you think they don't?

Ideas for Supplies ▼

- 1 package of yeast (check the expiration date)
- warm water
- 1 teaspoon sugar
- clear measuring cup

To investigate more, with an adult's permission, try making homemade bread and seeing how the dough behaves. You'll find one recipe at this website. Record your observations in your science journal.

 PBS bread bag

IT'S ALIVE!

Yeasts are single-cell eukaryotes and a type of fungus. They make up only about 1 percent of the fungi, but there are still approximately 1,500 types of yeast. Yeast reproduces asexually, meaning that a parent cell forms daughter cells that are just like it. The daughter cells start out as buds that grow, then they separate from the parent cell. Some yeasts are harmful, and we depend on others for our food. Yeast is the key ingredient in many breads. Bread yeast is called Saccharomyces cerevisiae.

- **Fill the measuring cup with ¼ cup of warm water.** Add the package of yeast, stirring it gently in the warm water.

- **Add 1 teaspoon of sugar and stir gently until dissolved.**

  - What do you see happening? Do you see bubbles? This is carbon dioxide that comes from the yeast eating the sugar.

  - After a while, does it look like the yeast mixture is growing? The yeast is reproducing and making more yeast and carbon dioxide. This process is called fermentation. This is why yeast is used to make bread. The yeast keeps working during the bread-making process, creating pockets in the dough, which causes it to expand. This process is what makes bread soft and light.

- **Try this experiment with cold water.** What do you observe? Can you explain why the temperature of the water would make a difference in how the yeast behaves?

Chapter 3 ▶

Growing Plants

SUNLIGHT IS VERY IMPORTANT TO PLANTS!

How do plant cells function to keep plants alive and healthy?

Plant cells have special organelles that aid in photosynthesis, which is the process of transforming light into usable energy.

Look outside the window. The chances are good that you'll see some kind of plant growing, whether you live in the country, the city, or even the desert. Plants grow pretty much everywhere except for the North and South Poles.

Plants are abundant and they've been around far longer than animals. Approximately 72 percent of the estimated 298,000 land plants have been classified, compared to only 12 percent of land animals and 7 percent of land fungi. Scientists have been classifying plants for more than 250 years. Plants also tend to remain in one place, unlike animals, which often hide when they feel threatened.

Scientists believe that plants evolved from green algae more than 500 million years ago. Skip ahead about 150 million years and much of the land by then was covered with forests of fern-like trees, pines, and ginkgos. It was a time when both plants and animals evolved in an explosion of new species. Flowering plants first grew about the time dinosaurs became extinct, 65 million years ago.

In the past 200 years, improving microscope technology has allowed scientists to see more and more of what was once impossible to see. During the 1800s, what did you look at with a new, improved microscope? After examining saliva, hair, and skin cells, what's next? If you're like the amateur and professional scientists of the 1800s, you realize that you have plenty of living organisms at your fingertips. Plants!

[Plants and algae were some of the first specimens scientists viewed in microscopes.]

Cell biology benefitted from the study of plant cells and many of the discoveries of the 1800s. Plant cells were readily available. They were easy to view due to their size and flexibility. Algae was also common in water samples, both in fresh water and in salt water.

Plant cells are eukaryotic organisms. They share similarities to animal cells, but what are the differences? And how do those differences affect other living organisms on Earth?

TYPES OF PLANT CELLS

Plants can be grouped into two categories, either nonvascular or vascular. Nonvascular plants are small plants, such as moss, that grow close to the ground, only 1 to 2 inches high. They are so short because they don't have a system for transporting water throughout their structure. Nonvascular plants live in shady, damp areas. These wet environments provide nonvascular plants with everything they need to survive and thrive.

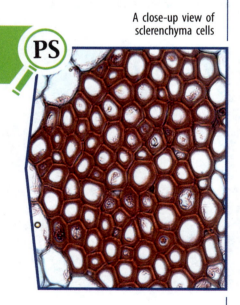

Sclerenchyma cells include fibers from plants, which are used to make certain types of thread and fabric, such as linen.

A close-up view of sclerenchyma cells

Vascular plants are more complex. They have vascular tissue, which forms roots, stems, and leaves. Vascular tissue provides structure to a plant. Their vascular tissue transfers water and food into the appropriate molecules for their growth and development.

A plant's roots, stems, and leaves are made up of plant cells. Like bacteria, plant cells have cell walls. But not all plant cells look the same. Scientists have discovered differences in the structures of the cell walls and protoplasts in plant cells. These differences led to the identification of three major classes of plant cells— parenchyma, collenchyma, and sclerenchyma.

Parenchyma cells provide the foundation for plant structure, function, and support. They are the most common type of plant cells. They store what a plant requires to live and make repairs when needed. Parenchyma cells are also where photosynthesis occurs.

Collenchyma cells support the plant as it grows in height. Because of this, they are typically found in the stem. The support is sometimes referred to as plastic support because the flexibility of many stems increase as collenchyma cells grow longer. This allows plants to bend without necessarily breaking. If you look at celery closely, you might notice the strings on the stalks. These are collenchyma cells.

Sclerenchyma cells also provide structure and support to plants. Unlike the other two types of cells, sclerenchyma cells die at maturity. It is at death that these cells are most useful because they support the plant without needing the care and maintenance that living cells need. The shells around nuts and seeds are made up of sclerenchyma cells.

PLANT CELL STRUCTURE

After studying plants with his microscope for some time, French researcher Charles-Francois Brisseau de Mirbel (1776–1854) proposed in 1809 that all plants are made up of cells. A pair of German botanists, Johann Heinrich Friedrich Link (1767–1851) and Karl Asmund Rudolphi (1771–1832), made another discovery soon afterward. Yes, plant cells have a plasma membrane, but they also have a wall around that membrane.

Plant cells are the only eukaryotic organisms with cell walls. The cell wall surrounds the plasma membrane, providing an extra layer of protection around the cell. It also allows the plant cell to hold more water, which it needs for growth and development.

Cell walls differ according to the type of cell. Parenchyma cells have thin primary walls. Collenchyma cells also have primary walls, but parts of the wall are thicker, where three or more cells have joined when plastids don't develop. Plastids are very important components in plant cells. They are responsible for photosynthesis and the storage of food.

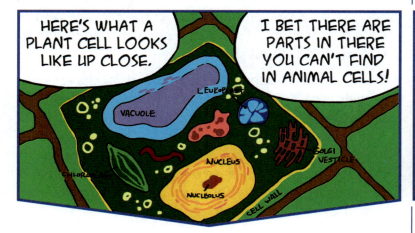

Plant cells tend to stay in one place, but there are exceptions. Some flowering plants produce gametes that use flagella to move.

COOL CONCEPT

While plant cells don't move, within a plant cell there is plenty of movement. Watch chloroplasts moving in a plant cell here.

microscope simulator

Unlike the other two cell types, sclerenchyma cells develop two cell walls. The secondary wall lies inside the primary one. Made of a polymer called lignin, which forms the woody tissue in a plant, the wall is hard and waterproof. This hardness makes it almost impossible for cell nutrients to pass through. This is why sclerenchyma cells lose their cytoplasm and die at maturity.

In addition to cell walls, plant cells contain other structures that animal cells don't have. Plant cells contain a centrally located vacuole, which is the largest part of the plant cell structure. In fact, it's so large that it pushes all the other organelles to the edges of the cell. The vacuole is a storage area for waste. It also contains water, sugars, and salts that keep leaves and stems healthy. In some plants, the vacuole contains pigments that make color for flowers, vegetables, and fruits. And when the vacuole contains plenty of water, it stretches the cell membrane tight and pushes the plant to stand tall.

Plant cells generally lack the filaments that other eukaryote cells use for movement. Plant cells don't need them because they stay in one location!

Plasmodesmata are the interstate highways for plant cells. These small protein tubes connect plant cells to each other so the cells can communicate and exchange information without moving.

Plants don't breathe, because the don't have lungs or gills. But they do respirate! Plants absorb oxygen and release carbon dioxide through stomata. These microscopic openings are found on the undersides of leaves. It's a common misconception that plants take in carbon dioxide and release oxygen through respiration. It's actually through photosynthesis, not respiration, that they release oxygen.

Plants must be careful not to lose too much water when its stomata are open. The loss of water is known as transpiration. Plants can minimize transpiration by opening stomata at times of the day when there is more humidity in the air, so less moisture escapes from the plant. If a plant becomes dehydrated, it can close its stomata to keep from losing more water.

One of the most important parts of the structure of a plant cell is chloroplasts. Both chloroplasts and mitochondria have inner and outer membranes. In 1881, Theodor Engelmann (1843–1909) discovered that photosynthesis occurs in the chloroplasts. Chloroplasts are organelles that convert light energy into chemical energy. This chemical energy is food for the plant, and the process of making it is photosynthesis.

PHOTOSYNTHESIS

Like many areas of cell science, gaining knowledge about photosynthesis has been a collaborative effort. In fact, 10 of the Nobel Prizes for chemistry have involved research on photosynthesis. Because photosynthesis is how plants make their own food and provide us with the oxygen we need to breathe, it is essential to all life.

As early as the seventeenth century, a Flemish scientist named Jan Baptist van Helmont (1580–1644) hypothesized that in order to grow, plants must get their food from other sources in addition to the soil. He assumed that water provided the nutrients. In the next century, a Dutch chemist named Jan Ingenhousz (1730–1799) showed that light is another necessary factor in plant survival.

In the early nineteenth century, Swiss physicist Nicolas-Theodore de Saussure (1767–1845) did some experiments on a willow tree. He wanted to know how plants receive nutrients.

The largest part of a plant cell is the vacuole. Because it takes up 80 to 90 percent of a plant cell's volume, it pushes other components of the cell toward the cell membrane.

PHOTOSYNTHESIS

How does the process of photosynthesis work? Check out this interactive video that originally aired on the *Nova* episode, "The Methuselah Tree."

Nova photosynthesis

He measured the exchange of gases of the willow tree and discovered that plants take in water and carbon dioxide. But they also release waste products they don't need. That waste product is oxygen gas.

By 1842, German physician Julius Robert von Mayer (1814–1878) put it all together. When a plant has enough water and carbon dioxide, the cells in the plant's leaves and stems convert light energy from the sun into chemical energy stored as carbohydrates in the form of glucose. The process is called photosynthesis and the chemical reaction produces oxygen gas. The chemical formula for photosynthesis is:

$6 CO_2$ (carbon dioxide) + $6 H_2O$ (water) + sunlight = $C_6H_{12}O_6$ (glucose) + $6 O_2$ (oxygen)

Photosynthesis takes place primarily in the leaves of a plant. Remember how plants breathe different gases in and out through the stomata? This gas exchange is the beginning of the process of photosynthesis.

[Learning about photosynthesis led to the discovery of a substance known as chlorophyll, which is found only in plants.]

MY PLANTS GET LOTS OF SUN, SO THEY'RE HAPPY AND HEALTHY!

SO HOW DO THEY TURN IT INTO ENERGY? IS IT LIKE FOOD?

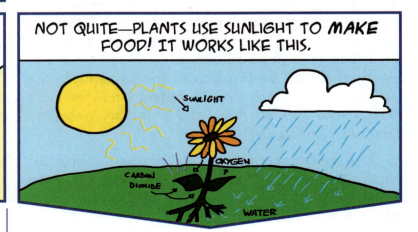

NOT QUITE—PLANTS USE SUNLIGHT TO *MAKE* FOOD! IT WORKS LIKE THIS.

By the 1860s, German scientist Julius von Sachs (1832–1897) determined that chlorophyll is what makes plants green. Furthermore, chlorophyll is found in only one location—the chloroplasts of a plant cell.

THE LIFE CYCLE OF PLANTS

Many plants begin life as seeds. When the seed germinates, a plant begins to grow and develop until it becomes a mature plant. Many mature plants then produce seeds, and the life cycle continues. Other plants reproduce by forming spores.

As with other eukaryotic cells, plant cells can divide using mitosis and meiosis. When you grow new plants from cuttings, the plants are reproducing from mitosis. Grass, strawberries, and ivy all grow this way.

Some plants, including many flowering plants, also use sexual reproduction, or meiosis, to reproduce. Plant cell meiosis can be more complicated than meiosis of animal cells.

During meiosis, plant cells divide by producing special cells, either gametes or spores. Spores are the reproductive cells of nonflowering plants, such as moss and ferns. They are haploid cells, meaning they have only one copy of each chromosome. When two haploid cells mix, they form a diploid organism with two of each copy of chromosome. In this way, the plant alternates between haploid and diploid with each generation.

Flowering plants depend on pollination to reproduce. The spores, or pollen, from a stamen (male part) must be transferred to a pistil (female part) of the flower. This transfer is done by bees, birds, wind, and even humans. If the pollination takes place in one plant, it's self-pollination. When it's between two separate plants, it's called cross-pollination.

JULIUS ROBERT VON MAYER

Julius Robert von Mayer (1814–1878) not only contributed to the theory of photosynthesis, he also developed the law of the conservation of energy, which states: Energy is neither created nor destroyed.

This is the first law of thermodynamics. The laws of thermodynamics are used in physics to explain the relationships of work and energy. The laws of thermodynamics are the rules by which everything in the universe is controlled. In living organisms, thermodynamics explain the chemical processes and energy that is present.

PLANT TISSUES

Organs are composed of tissues made from cells. While you have many organs, including the heart, liver, lungs, stomach, brain, and intestines, plants have only three. Those organs are the roots, stems, and leaves. Three different types of tissue make up the organs of a plant—dermal tissue, ground tissue, and vascular tissue.

Dermal tissue is the outer part of a plant, like the plant's skin. Ground tissue stores starches and provides structural support. It is also the tissue that performs photosynthesis. In what organ of plants do you think you would be most likely to find ground tissue? Where does photosynthesis take place?

Vascular tissue transports materials through the plant. Remember at the beginning of the chapter when we discussed nonvascular plants, such as moss? Since these plants have little to no vascular tissue, they can't transport nutrients. That's why nonvascular plants have to depend upon their environments.

ONLY IN PLANTS

Nitrogen is an important element that all cells need for survival. Animal cells get the nitrogen they need through organic forms, in the protein they consume. Unlike animal cells, plant cells don't need protein. Instead, they process inorganic forms of nitrogen for their needs.

[
Air is made up of about 78 percent nitrogen. When dissolved by rain, the nitrogen enters the soil. Plants then take in nitrogen through their roots.
]

320-MILLION-YEAR-OLD PLANT STEM CELLS

In 2016, Oxford University scientists discovered living plant stem cells in the fossilized root tip of a tree. These are the oldest-known plant cells, from 320 million years ago. Stem cells are cells responsible for growth and development. In plants, stem cells are most often found in the tips of shoots and roots. The discovery of the plant stem cells in such an old plant allows scientists to learn more about how roots developed at the time of the first global tropical wetland forests on Earth.

Water is essential for all of life, and plants, too, are dependent on it for survival. Without water, plants cannot perform photosynthesis, grow, and develop. Water also brings nutrients to the plant, including carbon, hydrogen, calcium, magnesium, nitrogen, oxygen, phosphorus, potassium, and sulfur. These elements are essential to life. Plants also benefit from smaller amounts of other elements, such as copper, iron, and zinc. These nutrients often exist in healthy soil from organic matter or artificially through man-made fertilizers.

The range and variety of plant life is immense. And plants are essential to all living organisms. Not only do plants provide the planet with oxygen, they also reduce carbon dioxide in the atmosphere. Plants slow down erosion and affect water levels and water quality. Plants are vital to the survival and evolution of animals. They provide us with food, shelter, and medicine.

We owe much of what we know in cell science to plant cells, the first multicellular organisms to be studied extensively. And as scientists look at the problem of trying to feed a growing population, plant cells will most definitely play a part. Although plants can make their own food, animal and human populations depend on plants to survive. Let's take a look at how animals function in the following chapter.

KEY QUESTIONS

- **What kinds of cells are found in plants, and what are their functions?**
- **How does the process of photosynthesis work?**
- **How is the survival of plants and animals connected?**

COOL CONCEPT

The blue whale is the largest animal in the world, but the largest living organism is the sequoia tree. These giant trees can grow up to 330 feet high.

MONOCOTS AND DICOTS

Flowering plants are divided into two groups, monocots and dicots. Monocots have flower parts in multiples of three and parallel leaf veins. Dicots have flower parts in multiples of four or five and leaf veins that do not follow a pattern. Monocots do not have secondary growth, which produces wood and bark, while dicots increase their diameter through this secondary growth. Think about the rings you see if you cut down a tree.

ELONGATING PLANT CELLS

You've learned that most plant cells don't move, but can they change shape? Can you change the shape of plant cells? Let's grow bean plants and see!

- **Poke two or three small holes in the bottom of several paper cups with a pencil or scissors.** Fill each cup with soil and plant two bean seeds in each plant cup.

- **You'll need sunlight to grow your bean plants.** To start your plants, indirect sunlight is best. Find a place where there is plenty of light during the day but it is not directly shining on your plants.

- **Your plants will also need regular watering.** Water the seeds after planting and when they become dry.

- **When the plants are 1 inch high, remove one plant from each pot.** Leave the healthiest plant in each cup. Mark two cups as "window" and place them in a sunny window.

- **For two of the other plants, apply auxin on the middle of the stem with a cotton swab.** Mark them "auxin" and leave in the window that doesn't receive direct light.

- **For the last two plants, mark as "indirect" for indirect lighting.** Place them in the window without direct light, next to the auxin sample.

- **Start a scientific method worksheet in your science journal.** Make predictions about the growth of the different plants. Observe your plants during the next few weeks, noting your observations of the growth of the plants in your notebook.

  - How do they differ?

  - Is the growth for any two sets of plants the same?

To investigate more, research auxin at the library or on the Internet. What is it? How does it affect plant growth? How does this substance help explain your results?

VOCAB LAB

Write down what you think each word means. What root words can you find for help?

chlorophyll, chloroplasts, collenchyma, dermal, lignin, parenchyma, photosynthesis, plasmodesmata, protoplasts, sclerenchyma, stomata, transpiration, vacuole, and **vascular.**

Compare your definitions with those of your friends or classmates. Did you all come up with the same meanings? Turn to the text and glossary if you need help.

EXAMINE PLANT CELLS

The pistil is the ovary, or female part, of a plant. Pollination leads to fertilization, which makes seeds for new plants. Carbohydrates and proteins that are stored in the seeds provide nutrition until the plant can form leaves and get chemical energy from the sun. When the seed is placed into the right conditions, it will germinate, or start the process of going from seed to plant. Can you achieve germination without soil?

- **Place cotton balls in a bowl.** Add room temperature water to bowl. Pour in enough to wet the cotton balls, but do not allow extra water in the bowl.

- **Sprinkle assorted seeds over the cotton.** Place bowl in sunlight. If cotton begins looking dry, add enough water to keep the cotton balls damp. Observe your seeds for several weeks.

  - Why do you think the seeds are able to germinate without soil?

  - How long do you think the seedlings will survive in a bowl of wet cotton?

> To investigate more, try the experiment in a sealable plastic bag instead of a bowl. What happens differently? Does the temperature of the water or amount of light make a difference? What other factors can you vary?

Chapter 4

Explore Animal Cells

How are animal cells different from plant cells?

While animal and plant cells share some similarities, the structures and behaviors of animal cells are unique. Different types of animal cells have different roles to play in the bodies they inhabit.

While plants and animals are multicellular organisms that share some cellular similarities, there are many important differences. In the large variety of animal and human cells, we see specialized cells ruled by differentiation. This means that the genes in each type of cell are customized to their locations and functions. For example, liver cells are programmed with enzymes to break down toxins. That is the function of the liver.

Research on animal cells lagged behind research on plant cells. Not only are animal cells smaller than plant cells, but in the past they were more difficult to prepare as samples. In 1830, a British entrepreneur named Joseph Jackson Lister (1786–1869) made things easier by designing a microscope capable of magnifying up to 400 times.

A few years later, scientists Jan Purkinje (1787–1869) and Gabriel Valentin (1810–1883) invented the microtome, a device that cuts thin, even slices of animal tissue for better viewing under a microscope. Both men were physiologists, which are scientists who look at how cells, tissues, and organisms function.

[
Since 1965, the invention of the scanning electron microscope (SEM) has allowed cell scientists to study whole samples without slicing.
]

Once scientists had a way to view animal cells, the discoveries began. Some studies confirmed hypotheses about animal cells that had been made based on plant cells, such as cell structure and cell division. That's what happened when German physiologist Theodor Schwann (1810–1882) compared his observations of animal cells with those of the plant cells studied by German botanist Matthias Jakob Schleiden (1804–1881). By comparing and sharing knowledge, they were able to develop theories about animal cells.

With animal cells, scientists had the opportunity to observe more complex multicellular organisms. Studying animal cells also meant learning more about humans. Our past, present, and future can be seen through the lens of cell science.

COOL CONCEPT

In some cases, illnesses are related to a problem in the programming of cells. Do you think studying cells could help to improve health?

IT'S A SMALL WORLD

Each year, Nikon sponsors a video competition called the Nikon Small World in Motion competition. The videos are of action caught under microscopes. The competition first began in 1975 to recognize people who use photography paired with a light microscope.

In 2011, the video competition was added. Photomicrographers from all over the world enter the competition.

See the 2016 winners here.

small world motion 2016 winners

COOL CONCEPT

The longest cells in the world reside in a giraffe's neck. These nerve cells can grow up to 10 feet long.

DIFFERENT TYPES OF ANIMAL CELLS

Animals are only one of the six kingdoms of living organisms, but there are believed to be approximately 7.7 million different animal species. When looked at on a cellular level, do you think all of these species are mostly alike or different? Do humans have anything in common with armadillos?

Unlike plant cells, animal cells come in all shapes and sizes. Sponges, the simplest multicellular organisms, have less than a dozen types of cells. Other animal species have significantly more. You, for example, have about 200 types.

Animals have skin cells, muscle cells, nerve cells, blood cells, and many more. Large numbers of cells join together to form tissue in animals. This tissue combines to form the various organs. For example, the heart is make up of blood, muscle, and other tissues.

In addition to having fewer types of cells, sponges are the only animals that don't have neurons.

photo credit: NOAA

The organs make up different systems in the body. Most animals have digestive, circulatory, nervous, respiratory, and immune systems. Each of these systems has a job that contributes to the health and survival of the animal.

Because different animal cells have different jobs to do, they can look and act very differently. Red blood cells look like tiny red saucers as they move around delivering oxygen and picking up carbon dioxide. They are quite different from the long, smooth, stretchy muscle cells that contain special proteins to control muscle contraction.

Nerve cells, usually called neurons, look and act very different from both muscle cells or blood cells. They resemble spider webs. The web shape makes sense when you consider that neurons must communicate with the other cells in the body.

Extensions known as axons extend from the center of the neuron like a wire. These axons carry electrical and chemical messages. A message starts as an electrical impulse. When it reaches the end of the axon, it triggers a chemical messenger called a neurotransmitter to send the message to a neighboring cell.

> In this way, a message from a neuron in your hand saying that it is touching a very hot surface gets to the brain very quickly. And the brain shoots a message back: "Immediately remove your hand from the very hot surface!"

Exactly how fast do these messages travel? Most neurons transmit messages about 250 miles per hour. This is because neurons are coated with a special fatty covering called myelin.

RED BLOOD CELLS

The red blood cells of birds and reptiles contain nuclei, but mature red blood cells in mammals lack nuclei. Red blood cells form from stem cells in the bone marrow, which is found in many of your bones. When they leave the bone marrow for the circulatory system, red blood cells must be flexible so they can squeeze into some tight places. A lack of a nucleus makes it possible for them to move through narrow channels. Also, red blood cells don't divide. They live about four to five months before they are shed and then replaced by more red blood cells from the bone marrow.

Myelin is a white substance that coats, protects, and insulates many nerve endings. It acts like insulation on a wire that helps to conduct electricity more effectively and faster.

Have you heard of photoreceptor cells? These are the neurons found in your eyes that help you see. Photoreceptor cells live in the retina of the eye. There are two types. Rod-shaped cells are more sensitive to light and are more plentiful—there are about 120 million in the human retina. They are active with light and dark shades, shape, movement, and peripheral vision. The second type of photoreceptor cells are the cones. These work to allow you to see color. Even in the same organ, two types of cells look different and do different jobs.

STRUCTURE AND FUNCTION

Just as in other organisms, animal cells are responsible for growth, movement, metabolism, and reproduction. While all cells contain cytoplasm, eukaryotic organisms such as plants and animals have internal membranes in their cells that separate the nucleus and other organelles from the cytoplasm.

Animal cells lack the cell wall of plant cells, but they have organelles that plant cells don't have, such as centrioles and lysosomes. Centrioles are small protein structures whose job is to help with cell division. In fact, when the centrioles can be seen, we know it's time for cell division. Lysosomes act like the digestive system of the cell. These organelles have enzymes that can break down materials, including proteins, carbohydrates, and lipids. Look back at the illustration on page 20.

Ribosomes differ between organisms. For example, in both bacteria and animal cells, ribosomes are made from protein and ribosomal RNA (rRNA), but the composition of molecules is different. This results in larger ribosomes in eukaryotic cells, such as those found in animals.

SVEDBERG UNITS

Ribosomes and other particles are measured by Svedberg units. This is how fast they "spin out" or drop to the bottom of a centrifuge tube. A centrifuge is a rapidly spinning device that separates parts by their density. It is used to study different parts of the cell. The larger, dense particles fall faster, while less dense particles take longer to separate out. Svedberg units tell scientists the relative sizes of different parts of the cell, including ribosomes.

Proteins attach themselves to the rough endoplasmic reticulum. Both the rough endoplasmic reticulum and the smooth endoplasmic reticulum are components of the endomembrane system of eukaryotic cells. In the endomembrane system, all membrane-bound organelles exchange membrane material and are highly interactive with each other. The system is similar to how a post office works. Other parts of this system are the Golgi apparatus, peroxisomes, and vesicles.

Proteins are sorted in the Golgi apparatus. Peroxisomes use molecular oxygen to oxidize organic molecules. Vesicles have a variety of functions, the main one being to shuttle molecules from one organelle to another and even to the membrane of the cell.

ENERGIZED

Cells need energy. This energy is what makes cell function and cell repair possible. Cells get some energy from a set of processes known as cellular respiration. Cellular respiration happens in organelles called mitochondria. When cells need more energy, they call on mitochondria to deliver. Mitochondria break down nutrients to create energized molecules that power cells.

During cellular respiration, chemical reactions take place to break down food molecules. These chemical reactions that are needed for survival are known together as metabolism. Breaking down a food molecule such as glucose is done through a reaction such as this:

$$C_6H_{12}O_6 + O_2 \rightarrow 6\ CO_2 + 6\ H_2O + energy$$

Can you interpret this chemical equation?

Glucose ($C_6H_{12}O_6$) combines with oxygen gas (O_2) to create carbon dioxide (CO_2), water (H_2O), and energy. Energy is stored in ATP (adenosine triphosphate).

CHEMICAL EQUATIONS

Chemical equations give us lots of information. First, they tell use what substances are being used up and what is being made. They also tell us the ratio of the substances. A chemical equation can explain the consequences of the reactions. Like mathematical equations, chemical equations must be balanced.

For example, look at
$$2H_2 + O_2 \rightarrow 2H_2O$$

No doubt you recognize that H_2O on the right side of the equation is water. And you can probably figure out that H_2 is hydrogen and O_2 is oxygen. But what is the number 2 in front on the chemical symbols? It's a coefficient that gives the number of molecules used in the reactions. So two molecules of hydrogen and one molecule of oxygen produces two molecules of water.

ATP is what a cell needs to transport energy from food molecules to where it's needed most, just as the gas in your car is needed to make the car go where you need it to. ATP helps power other processes and reactions in the cell.

The process of how cells use energy is defined by the laws of thermodynamics, particularly the first two laws.

- **The first law of thermodynamics:** Energy can't be created or destroyed. For example, chemical energy from food is converted into a different kind of energy, kinetic energy, allowing animals to breathe and move.

- **The second law of thermodynamics:** Spontaneous chemical reactions increase the disorder of an isolated system. An example of this is when a molecule such as glucose moves from areas of high concentration to low concentration. Energy is constantly being converted in cells and systems, but some of that energy is lost during the conversion process. So not all of that chemical energy (glucose) from food directly translates to cell functions of breathing and movement. Some of it is lost as heat.

MEIOSIS JOINS MITOSIS

Animal cells can divide in two different ways—mitosis and meiosis. Like other eukaryotes, most animal cells divide by the process of mitosis. Human cells may divide up to 50 times before dying.

Unlike plant cells, which have a cell wall, a band of actin microfilaments forms in the middle of the animal cell during mitosis. Then it tightens and pinches off two new cells.

THE SCIENCE OF BEGINNING

Marcello Malpighi (1628–1694) was an Italian scientist with an immense curiosity about the development of living things. Early in his career, he focused on animal cells, particularly frogs. He discovered various systems within animals, such as taste buds and capillaries. But his biggest focus was on early development. He wondered what developmental stages occur after fertilization. This early development is called the embryo stage. Malpighi published a book on the early development of chicks, from the time of fertilization to the fetal stage. He is considered the "father of embryology."

The type of cell division that provides living organisms with their genetic makeup comes from meiosis. Meiosis was first discovered about a hundred years ago. This is the process of gamete formation and sexual reproduction. Two divisions take place that reduce the chromosomes by half and produce four gametes from one parent cell. For example, in humans, one cell ready to divide contains 92 chromosomes, which splits into two daughter cells containing 46 chromosomes. Then meiosis further splits each daughter cell into two gametes that contain only 23 chromosomes each.

> Mitosis takes place throughout a multicellular organism, but meiosis occurs only in the ovaries, to produce egg cells, and in the testes, to produce sperm cells.

Here's how reproduction works with these cells. During ovulation in a female's body, an egg cell is released. If it meets a sperm cell, which is produced in a male's body, they combine to form a zygote. This process is known as fertilization. The zygote begins to divide and the ball of cells resulting from fertilization is first called an embryo and later a fetus. This is how YOU began!

CELL SCIENCE CONTROVERSY

Cell science is fascinating, but it's not without controversy. One of those controversies involves the use of animals for research. These animals can include mice, fish, rats, rabbits, guinea pigs, hamsters, farm animals, birds, cats, dogs, mini-pigs, monkeys, and chimpanzees. Science sometimes uses lab animals for research and experimentation in the quest to develop everything from cosmetics to medicines.

When a sperm cell and an egg cell combine, they become a zygote.

Understanding how a disease begins and spreads can be helpful in discovering cures. For example, lab animals have been used to better understand how tumors develop. New therapies that target abnormal cancer cells are being tested every year. These tests are often performed on animals before they are tested on humans.

Acute lymphoblastic leukemia is a type of cancer that often strikes children. In the early 1960s, only 4 percent of children survived it. Through research and testing, some of which happened on animals, treatments were developed. Today, 80 percent of children survive acute lymphoblastic leukemia. This is one example of how studying cells and testing therapies can lead to great strides in improving the health of humans.

Lab animals are also used by scientists who are working to discover new therapies to combat HIV and AIDS and medicines for heart disease, strokes, seizure disorders, and diabetes. Other research focuses on vaccines that will defend us against biological terrorism. What do you think about using animals in lab research?

Sometimes, scientists are able to use animal cell cultures, which are cells that are kept alive in a lab. No harm comes to live animals through this method.

The Adaptability of Cells

Bacteria and archaea may be able to live in any conditions, but that adaptability to harsh environments doesn't extend to animals. Or does it? Some animals can exist in extreme conditions, too. There are Arctic flies that can live in temperatures of -76 degrees Fahrenheit (-60 degrees Celsius). Insects and spiders produce an antifreeze that keeps their bodies from freezing. For some species of amphibians, more than half the water in their bodies is ice. Amphibians go into a type of hibernation. As the animal's body freezes, the cells of the animal squeeze out water and it is replaced with an antifreeze-type mixture of sugars and sugar alcohols. Only water outside of the cells can freeze, but not the individual cells.

Three aging northern white rhinos are all that remain on Earth.

What if experiments on animals could save a species, or many species, from becoming extinct? There are more than 44,000 endangered plant and animal species on Earth. Approximately 16,938 species are in critical danger of becoming extinct.

> Scientists are looking at cell science to save some of these species from disappearing. The northern white rhino is one of those threatened animals.

Researchers have collected white rhino egg cells. Frozen sperm cells are available from the San Diego Frozen Zoo. Scientists plan to try in vitro fertilization by combining the egg and sperm cells in the lab and then transferring the embryo to the uterus of a female rhino.

Cell science might be used to find other possible solutions to save an animal species from extinction. These solutions include cloning or using stem cells.

HELLO, DOLLY!

On July 5, 1996, scientists in a Scotland lab did something that no one had done before. They successfully cloned a living animal, a sheep they named Dolly. Dolly was created when scientists removed DNA from an adult sheep and implanted it into an egg through a process called nuclear transfer. The resulting baby sheep was the exact genetic copy of the adult sheep, as opposed to an individual that is genetically different due to the blending of the two parents' genes.

The first successful cloning of an animal created both excitement and fear. Some people questioned how far it would go. Would people be cloned?

SAN DIEGO FROZEN ZOO

One of the most popular zoos in the world is California's San Diego Zoo. Approximately 5 million people visit the thousands of animals that live there each year. But behind the scenes, away from visitors, even more species are housed. The San Diego Frozen Zoo contains more than 10,000 living cell cultures. Some represent extinct or soon-to-be extinct cell lines. The collection is being used in conservation efforts and wildlife medicine. Learn more here.

San Diego frozen zoo

Dolly the sheep died at age six from a lung infection commonly found in animals kept indoors.

CHIMERA STUDIES

On August 4, 2016, the National Institutes of Health (NIH) announced that the agency might soon allow experiments that add human stem cells to animal embryos, creating an organism that is part animal and part human. Called chimera studies, the experiments would use human pluripotent stem cells, which can be turned into any type of tissue. Scientists believe this method could help them learn more about human development and disease models. Potentially, it could also be used to grow human organs for transplants. Before such experiments proceed, the NIH plans to develop extra review measures.

Nuclear transfer has had limited applications, and there are no plans to use it or any other method to clone humans. Instead, cloning gave birth to new ideas and technology. Cell scientist Shinya Yamanaka (1952–) of Japan was spurred by the ideas and techniques of cloning to develop stem cells from adult cells.

[
Stem cells are very special because they have the ability to develop into a number of different cells, so they offer many possibilities to be used in different ways.
]

Today, cloning is limited to agricultural purposes. In the United States, cloning is mainly used for breeding purposes in cows, goats, and pigs. In 2015, the European Parliament voted to ban cloning animals for food.

Humans are animals, so human cells are animal cells. But just as there is diversity among plants, there is diversity among animals. Human cell science takes on an added importance for many of us, because after all, we're studying human life.

KEY QUESTIONS

- Why did animal cell research lag behind plant cells?
- Can plant and animal cells function without sunlight?
- How do animal cells differ from plant cells?
- What are some of the controversies of cell science and research?

ANIMAL CELLS

Although plants and animals are both eukaryotic organisms, we've discovered that there are differences between plants and animal cells. Are there are also differences between the cells of different animals? The largest known cell is an ostrich egg. Other than size, would the egg cell of a fly look any different?

- **Research the different types of animal cells and recreate them as drawings, paintings, or models.**

- **What types of materials make sense to use for the different types of cells?** How much cell variety can you find in one organ?

- **Create models that show how different cells function in different ways.** Here are some of the cells you will find:

  - Bone cells
  - Cartilage cells
  - Muscle cells
  - Nerve cells (neurons)
  - Oocytes (eggs)

  - Photoreceptor cells
  - Red blood cells
  - Skin cells
  - Sperm cells
  - White blood cells

To investigate more, create a comic book with different types of animal cells as your characters. How do they interact with each other? What do they need from each other? Create scenarios that offer the cell characters a chance to describe their structures and functions.

VOCAB LAB

Write down what you think each word means. What root words can you find for help?

bone marrow, cellular respiration, cloning, embryo, metabolism, microtome, photoreceptor, ribosomes, thermodynamics, and **stem cell.**

Compare your definitions with those of your friends or classmates. Did you all come up with the same meanings? Turn to the text and glossary if you need help.

OSMOSIS

In a cell, nutrients must be able to get into a cell and wastes need to come out of the cell. The cell membrane acts like a filter so only the right things move in and out of the cell through tiny openings in the membrane. One of the most important molecules that needs to move in and out of the cells is water. This movement of water is called osmosis.

If you've ever looked at an onion layer under a microscope, you'll see rectangular boxes stacked on each other. These boxes are the cells of the onion. Let's see how osmosis works on a slice of onion.

- **Pour the warm water into the bowl.** Add the salt and stir until dissolved.

- **Add the onion slice to the salty water.** Let the onion remain in the water for a few hours.

- **When you return to the bowl with the onion, what do you see?**

  - Has the amount of water changed?

  - What does the onion look like?

  - What is the effect of osmosis on onion cells?

To investigate more, what happens if you returned the onion slice to regular water? Can you think of other objects other than an onion to try this experiment with? Remember to log what you see in your science notebook.

Chapter 5 ▶

The Human Side of Cell Science

How does cell science affect humans?

Through studying cells, especially the DNA of cells, we can make changes to the way we treat illness and injury, grow food, reproduce, solve crimes, and many other human activities!

Cell growth and division works the same in you as it does in your pet dog or cat or in the elephants at the zoo. Humans are animals with eukaryotic cells like other animals. But when we start applying cell science to humans, it takes on new importance and possibilities.

Perhaps one of the more interesting explorations of cell science in the twentieth century was the part it plays in heredity. Why does one family have several members that are left-handed and another family has members that are only right-handed? Why are your eyes blue and your friend's eyes green?

These questions and many more can be answered by studying cells and DNA. And studying DNA isn't useful only for people who are trying to track their family gene pool. Toward the end of the last century, medicine and forensic science were changed forever by a new understanding of DNA.

CELL PROCESSES IN HUMANS

Have you ever had a paper cut? Maybe it stung a little bit, but chances are you quickly forgot about it. After all, these usually disappear in a couple of days. But a huge amount of cellular activity is required to heal that tiny cut!

First, nerve cells known as nociceptors signal the brain that there's been an accident. The brain sends a message to cells that it's time to register pain. Cells in the blood vessels are called to the wound, bringing blood with hemoglobin. The hemoglobin brings oxygen to the wound.

Another signal goes to the nervous system calling for platelets, another cell type found in the blood. When the platelets in the blood arrive, they clump together at the wound to stop bleeding. Platelets summon other cells and proteins to protect the wound and start the rebuilding process. About an hour later, white blood cells called neutrophils finish cleaning the wound.

Within 24 hours, other white blood cells called macrophages arrive to vacuum up the neutrophils and any remaining potentially damaging substances. Rebuilding starts. Fibroblasts cover the wound and start a foundation. Skin cells grow layer by layer, forming a gauze-like mesh, getting rid of dead cells as they finish the rebuilding process. Eventually, there is no sign of that small cut!

GENETICS

Gregor Mendel (1822–1884) was an Austrian monk who liked to conduct experiments to answer his many questions about life. He lived and worked in what today is the Czech Republic.

COOL CONCEPT

Human cells have receptors on their membranes that tell the other cells what they are, like identification badges. Receptors also allow cells to respond to specific extracellular signals, like hormones.

BLOOD CELLS

There are three types of blood cells in humans: red blood cells, white blood cells, and platelets. Red blood cells carry oxygen throughout the body. White blood cells are the body's defense system, ready to defend against foreign invaders. We call them white blood cells because they are colorless. Platelets are in charge of clotting. They are like a drain plug that plugs up blood vessels when they are damaged.

COOL CONCEPT

Gregor Mendel's genetics experiments actually looked at seven different traits of pea plants: plant height, seed shape, seed color, seed coat color, pod shape, pod color, and flower position.

Mendel observed the traits of pea plants, including their height and the shape and colors of the pods and seeds. He knew that peas could be green or yellow, smooth or wrinkled. But what determined their color and the texture of their skin?

Mendel hypothesized that traits were being passed from one generation of peas to the next. He found that when he crossed a green pea plant with a yellow pea plant, the entire next generation of plants was yellow. Yet the generation of yellow pea plants produced green pea plants, on average, one out of every four times.

Mendel decided that smooth, yellow peas were dominant traits in the pea plants. Green and wrinkled peas were recessive traits.

> Mendel believed he could predict the appearance of pea plants by identifying dominant and recessive traits.

Mendel published the results of his work in 1866 but received little attention for it. In 1900, after his death, agricultural researchers uncovered his work and verified his results. Today, Gregor Mendel is considered the father of genetics because his groundbreaking work led to three laws, or principles, of inheritance.

- **Principle of segregation:** Two members of a gene pair—the copy from your mother and the copy from your father—separate from each other during the formation of gametes in meiosis. Half the gametes carry one allele, and the other half carry the other allele. Alleles are different variations of a gene, such as blond hair and brown hair. So, if one parent has brown eyes, identified as BB, the BB becomes B + B, separating, or segregating, so that each can go with an egg or sperm cell.

- **Principle of independent assortment:** Genes for different traits sort independently of one another during the formation of gametes. We have genes that determine many different things: eye color, height, hair color, etc. But the genes that make up each of these traits will separate, or segregate, independently of the other traits.

- **Principle of dominance:** One of the factors for a pair of inherited traits will be dominant and the other recessive, unless both factors are recessive. For example, brown is a dominant hair color (B) and blond is recessive (b). If an individual has one B (brown) allele and one b (blond) allele, the hair color will be brown, since brown is a dominant gene.

It was American Walter Sutton who came up with the word "gene" to describe a unit of inheritance. This unit is a phenotype, or observable characteristic, such as eye or hair color or dominant hand use.

WHAT IS DNA AND WHY IS IT IMPORTANT?

In 1869, Swiss scientist Friedrich Miescher (1844–1895) extracted a chemical from white blood cells and called it nuclein. The name was changed to nucleic acid and later to deoxyribonucleic acid, or DNA. Although the name changed, the substance didn't.

[
Miescher and his contributions were largely forgotten until scientists had better microscopes to understand the significance of Miescher's discovery.
]

BARBARA McCLINTOCK (1902–1992)

Many scientists applied Mendel's work to other living organisms. One of those scientists was Barbara McClintock, who studied plant genetics. What Gregor Mendel did with peas, Barbara McClintock did with maize, or corn. After observing patterns of colorization in kernels within generations of maize, she suggested that genes could move within and between chromosomes. Like Lynn Margules in Chapter 1, no one believed McClintock until techniques of the late 1970s and early 1980s confirmed her theory. McClintock was awarded a Nobel Prize in 1983. For more on McClintock's work, go to this website.

🔎 dnaftb animation mcclintock

Scientists began focusing on DNA in the early twentieth century. What did it look like? What was its function? Russian biochemist Phoebus Levene (1869–1940) proposed that DNA was made up of nucleotides. He identified the components of a nucleotide as a nitrogen base (now known as adenine, cytosine, thymine, and guanine), a five-carbon sugar, and a phosphate group.

Scientists suspected that the hereditary material that Mendel first wrote about was contained in DNA. In the 1940s, scientists at the Rockefeller Institute for Medical Research were able to prove it.

> Once it was confirmed that DNA plays a significant part in genetics, scientists wanted to know all they could about this molecule, starting with its structure and what it looks like.

Erwin Chargaff (1905–2002) expanded on the work of Levene and the Rockefeller Institute by looking at the chemistry of nucleic acids. The sugars were identified as either ribose or deoxyribose. Ribose is used to make RNA and deoxyribose makes DNA.

Additionally, there are two types of nitrogen bases—pyrimidines and purines. The pyrimidines are cytosine (C), thymine (T), and uracil (U). Purines are adenine (A) and guanine (G). Later, it was discovered that RNA doesn't contain any thymine and DNA doesn't contain any uracil. These four nitrogen bases are the building blocks of DNA.

Chargaff was also able to show that while the composition of DNA varies, something always remains the same. The amount of adenine is always the same as the amount of thymine, and the same goes for cytosine and guanine. This equality became known as Chargaff's rule.

Physicist Maurice Wilkins (1916–2004) of Kings College in London was working on capturing an image of DNA. Working in the same lab on another DNA project was chemist Rosalind Franklin (1920–1958). She was experimenting with X-ray diffraction to produce detailed images of various molecules and their structures. In 1952, she produced an image of the molecules that make up DNA. Wilkins shared her image with American biologist James Watson (1928–) and British biophysicist Francis Crick (1916–2004).

Watson and Crick had been working on identifying the structure of DNA. When they saw the image Franklin had created, it was the "aha" moment they had been searching for.

For Watson and Crick, it was like putting a puzzle together. They started with cardboard cutouts to represent the components of DNA. They made a molecule with two strands of nucleotides that run in opposite directions. The twisting ladder shape is called a double helix. Adenine (A) is on one strand and linked to thymine (T) on the other strand by two chemical bonds of hydrogen. Likewise, guanine (G) is linked to cytosine (C), but with three hydrogen bonds instead of two. These linked nucleotides have a sugar-phosphate backbone.

COOL CONCEPT

One of the Rockefeller Institute's noted scientists was Marie Maynard Daly (1921–2003), the first African American woman to receive a doctorate in chemistry in the United States. While at the institute, she studied how proteins are produced and organized in the cell. She was also interested in the composition and metabolism of components of the cell nucleus.

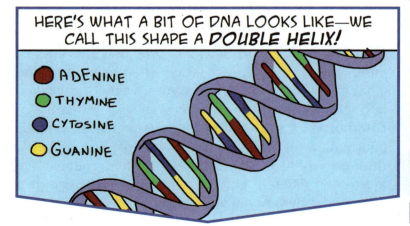

HERE'S WHAT A BIT OF DNA LOOKS LIKE—WE CALL THIS SHAPE A *DOUBLE HELIX!*

- ADENINE
- THYMINE
- CYTOSINE
- GUANINE

CODED IN THAT TWIST IS THE INFORMATION THAT MAKES US WHO WE ARE!

Watson, Crick, and Wilkins won the Nobel Prize in 1962 for their work in discovering the DNA structure. The Nobel Prize is given out only to living scientists.

> Rosalind Franklin did not receive one for her part, although without her contributions, it's questionable whether the men would have won the esteemed science prize.

She had died four years earlier of cancer, a disease that scientists have discovered a lot about in part due to her pioneering work in DNA research.

TIE IT ALL TOGETHER

DNA is the hereditary material that all living organisms contain. In eukaryotic organisms, DNA is found mainly in the cell nucleus and a smaller amount is found in the mitochondria.

During reproduction, the genetic material of the largest human cell, the egg, combines with the genetic material of the smallest human cell, the sperm. The egg and sperm cells are gametes, which are haploid cells that have each received half of the usual number of chromosomes during meiosis.

Once the connection between DNA and the laws of inheritance were known, scientists began applying what they knew to chromosomes. DNA is packaged into chromosomes. A human cell has 23 pairs of chromosomes, each with hundreds of genes. Genetic information is passed from parent to offspring through these chromosomes. If two genes are located on different chromosomes, they will segregate independently among offspring.

Since Watson and Crick provided the world with a visual model of DNA, knowledge of DNA has continued to grow. During the next several decades, scientists learned much more about genes and the special substance called DNA, as well as its applications for medicine, technology, and industry.

THE CHANGING FACE OF CRIMINOLOGY

Crime shows have long been a favorite of television audiences, but in the past 20 years, there has been a big change in how crimes are solved. Now, forensic evidence and laboratories play a large part in solving crimes, both on television and in real life. And it's all because of DNA.

Criminal investigators can use DNA evidence from human cells to solve crimes. Here's how it works. Samples of evidence are collected at crime scenes. Some samples are obvious, such as blood. Others might come from anything a person has worn or touched, which leaves behind skin, hair, or other tissue. Investigators look at what shouldn't be there, such as DNA from another person.

Human DNA's code of four nitrogen bases—adenine, cytosine, guanine, and thymine—make up about 3 billion building blocks. Approximately 99 percent of the sequences of these building blocks are the same for all humans.

[It's the 1 percent that marks the differences between each human.]

HOW MANY CHROMOSOMES?

Although chromosomes are mostly organized the same, the number of chromosomes varies greatly among organisms. You can't predict the number of chromosomes based solely on an organism's size. With 46 chromosomes, you have more than the eight chromosomes of a fruit fly. But a dog has you both beat with 78 chromosomes.

Oxytricha trifallax

A little-known protist living in ponds has 15,600 chromosomes. The Oxytricha trifallax is a single-cell organism about a fourth of a millimeter long. The Oxytricha trifallax has two nuclei with thousands of "nanochromosomes" in its micronucleus.

DNA recovered from a crime scene can be compared to victims and suspects. The comparison, or analysis, looks at markers in sequences of DNA. If the suspect is unknown, investigators can compare the samples to others in the FBI National DNA Index System (NDIS), which was created in 1998 and is part of the Combined DNA Index System (CODIS). More than 10 million DNA profiles are in the system, which has helped in approximately 170,000 investigations.

DNA has been used to identify suspects and solve crimes, as well as to reverse prison sentences. Since 1989, more than 300 people have been exonerated for crimes they did not commit because of newly analyzed DNA evidence.

GENOMIC LIBRARY

A complete set of DNA is a called a genome. Scientists have discovered that the human genome contains about 3.2 billion base pairs of DNA that encode approximately 30,000 genes. This is less than one-third of what scientists had previously estimated. Why do you think we have less DNA than we originally thought? We know the function of slightly more than half of all human genes.

What if there were a gene library that contained the genomes of all organisms? Believe it or not, it is happening. This process, called sequencing, determines the exact orders, or sequences, of the base pairs.

In 1976, the first complete DNA genome was sequenced, of a virus with one chromosome and 3,569 base pairs. In 1995, the first bacteria genome was sequenced. It has 1.8 million base pairs. In 1998, the first animal genome to be sequenced was that of the nematode worm, which has half as many chromosomes as humans and 100 million base pairs.

The Human Genome Project started in late 1990 as a cooperative effort among scientists in the United States, Great Britain, France, Germany, Japan, and China. It was completed on April 14, 2003. It was found that the human genome contains around 3 billion base pairs in the 23 pairs of chromosomes in our cells. Each chromosome can contain thousands of genes, and each gene makes an average of three proteins.

> In this new frontier of science, the possibilities of genomic science are like an unmapped wilderness waiting to be discovered and conquered.

The human body contains a wondrous collection of cells. Their structures fit their functions. And within the nucleus of our cells is literally the blueprint of life—DNA. You would not build a house without plans, just hammering things together randomly. Life is not built randomly either. We know DNA is central to life, but can it be used to improve life?

KEY QUESTIONS

- What do cells tell us about basic processes of life, including life, death, and reproduction?
- How are cells like building blocks?
- Many people believe Rosalind Franklin didn't get the recognition she deserved for her work on the structure of DNA. Do you think if she were working today that would still be a problem? Why or why not?
- Why is understanding DNA important?

You have about 37.2 trillion cells in your body. This is an estimate, because how could you count all the cells in a human body? Many of your cells measure only about 1/1000 of an inch.

GENETIC PREDICTIONS

The science of genetics has many applications. One of those is predicting inherited traits. Genetics looks at the mathematical probability of inheritance. A simple tool for looking at mathematical probability is the Punnett square, developed by Reginald C. Punnett in 1905.

- **A Punnett square looks something like this.**

	MOTHER SHEEP (Ww)	
	W	w
FATHER SHEEP (ww) w	Ww	ww
w	Ww	ww

- **The 'W' represents wool color.** The mother sheep has white wool, which is a dominant trait. However, one of her parents had black wool, a recessive trait. So, her allele is represented as Ww. The father is a black sheep. Black wool is a recessive trait, so the alleles can only be ww.

- **If this pair of sheep had four offspring, two would receive a dominant white wool trait and therefore have white wool (Ww).** The other two would receive two recessive genes for black wool and be black sheep (ww).

- **Let's see what happens when we add another trait, such as eye color.** Brown is the dominant eye color for sheep and can be represented as EE or Ee. Blue is a recessive eye color and can only be ee.

	MOTHER SHEEP (Wwee)			
	We	We	we	we
wE	WwEe	WwEe	wwEe	wwEe
we	Wwee	Wwee	wwee	wwee
wE	WwEe	WwEe	wwEe	wwEe
we	Wwee	Wwee	wwee	wwee

Left-side label: **FATHER SHEEP (wwEe)**

- **The results are:**
  - Four sheep: White wool, brown eyes (WwEe)
  - Four sheep: Black wool, brown eyes (wwEe)
  - Four sheep: White wool, blue eyes (Wwee)
  - Four sheep: Black wool blue eyes (wwee)

- **Research various dominant and recessive traits.**
Create your own Punnett squares to predict the
outcomes of traits. Here's a Punnett square to get
you started.

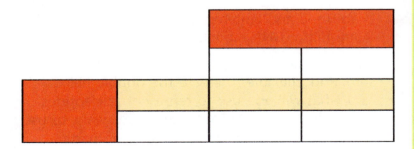

To investigate more,
create a list of human
traits with your
classmates. Discuss
whether they are all
hereditary traits. Which
are dominant and which
are recessive? The Tech
Museum of Innovation
is an interesting place
to start your
research.

the Tech ask363

You can also try out
"What Color Eyes Would
Your Children
Have" here.

the Tech what
color

DNA MODEL

It's often said that a picture is worth a thousand words. This was quite true when Watson and Crick first set eyes on Rosalind Franklin's X-ray photographs of DNA. Suddenly, the structure of DNA made sense and the scientists rushed to create a model and publish their findings.

- **When the structure of DNA was first introduced, it was shown as a twisting ladder, called a double helix.** The rungs on each side are the nucleotides, and hydrogen bonds are the steps that link them.

- **Look for materials that you can use to make your own DNA model.**

  - Watson and Crick used cardboard. You can find a paper template to print and fold at this website.

   CSIRO paper DNA

  - Genome British Columbia has published instructions for an edible DNA model.

  British Columbia edible DNA

  - YouTube and Pinterest are full of DNA models.

- **What materials will you use?** You'll need something flexible to create the double helix. And what will you use to represent nucleotides and hydrogen bonds? You might also want to use different colors to distinguish between parts.

To investigate more, look at the different sequences that can be made with the four nitrogen bases. Remember the base pairings of the nitrogen bases. How many sequences can you come up with?

Chapter 6 ▶

Cells Impact Medicine and Agriculture

BAD GENES CAN GET PASSED DOWN, TOO.

How does our knowledge about cells affect the way we treat illness and produce food?

New discoveries in cell science make it possible for scientists to treat diseases in new ways, and even alter the way we grow vegetables and produce meat to eat. We are learning more every year.

As scientists have learned more and more about DNA, they have discovered many ways to use this knowledge. If certain chromosomes determine appearance, could they also have something to do with diseases? Could this be particularly true for diseases that appear to run in families, such as sickle cell anemia and cystic fibrosis?

And what about plant diseases? Some crops, such as corn and cotton, are susceptible to plant infestations, fungi, or disease. Could the DNA of these crops be manipulated to produce plants with an immunity to disease or plants that are hardy enough to fight pests?

Do you remember the water mold that destroyed potato crops during the 1800s? Events would have been different if scientists had the tools and the knowledge to produce resistant potato plants at the time. If some diseases are inherited in people or animals or plants, should science do something to change the outcome?

HELLO, HELA

A woman named Henrietta Lacks has made an unusual contribution to cell science. She was a poor African American woman from a long line of Virginian tobacco farmers. When she turned 30, Lacks started feeling sick. She finally went to Johns Hopkins Hospital in Baltimore, where she was diagnosed with cervical cancer. She died from the disease in 1951.

Before she died, scientists took a sample of tissue cells during a biopsy of her tumor and created a cell culture that could grow in an artificial environment. Lacks and her family never knew about this. The cells were labeled HeLa, after the first letters in Lacks's name.

With this culture, scientists created the first human cell line. A cell line is a cell culture that keeps producing cells indefinitely. HeLa cells have been preserved through freezing. They have multiplied and been divided among researchers. HeLa cells are still used today for research.

Most cell scientists got their start with HeLa cells like these.

photo credit: National Institutes of Health

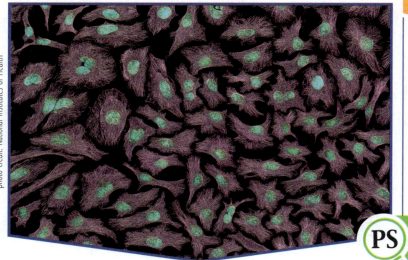

CANCER RESEARCHERS

As an African American student, Jewel Plummer Cobb (1924–2017) had to battle discrimination throughout her education. This is why she had long dedicated some of her time to helping and encouraging minority science students. With a PhD in cell physiology, Plummer Cobb was one of the leading cancer researchers in the United States and her work in testing drugs on cancer cells has provided successful treatment options for many. Learn more about her from the Connecticut Women's Hall of Fame here.

🔍 Jewel Plummer Cobb Tribute Film

Scientists learned from HeLa cells that humans have 23 pairs of chromosomes.

The year after the death of Lacks, a polio vaccine was tested on HeLa cells. Polio is a highly infectious disease that attacks the nervous system, mainly infecting children under the age of five. Thousands of people used to contract the disease every year. Some polio victims died, and many were paralyzed for the rest of their lives. Others could only breathe through a ventilation device known as an iron lung while they were recovering.

> After the introduction of the tested vaccine, polio cases dropped 99 percent in the United States. The last case of polio in this country was in 1979. Cases have decreased in most areas of the world as well.

In addition to the polio vaccine, HeLa cells were used to develop procedures for gene mapping, in vitro fertilization, and cloning. They have furthered scientists' knowledge of cancer and human immunodeficiency virus (HIV). HeLa cells have even been to space!

MEDICAL ADVANCES

Medical advances from cell science are plentiful and significant. Scientists have learned to identify different genetic markers for mutations that result in various diseases. Genetic testing on fetuses provides early detection and sometimes even treatment of diseases and conditions before a baby is born. Adults can have genetic testing to determine if they've inherited certain conditions or if they are carriers of conditions that might affect their children.

Many diseases are caused by cell mutations. Cancer, the second leading cause of death in the United States, after heart disease, is caused by uncontrolled cell growth and reproduction. For some reason, these cells don't respond to normal growth controls, and instead take over systems in the body.

[Cancer is actually a group of diseases that can be caused by lifestyle decisions, such as smoking, and internal factors, such as random mutations.]

Recent cancer research has suggested that certain genes, called oncogenes, might cause this uncontrolled cell production. Oncogenes are proteins with mutations that promote cell division even if it's not supposed to be happening. The switch for cell reproduction gets stuck in the "on" position. Tumor cells develop and send signals to healthy cells to produce new blood vessels around the cancerous cells.

Experiments in medications that slow or stop the growth of cancer cells have been promising. For example, a protein called endostatin has reduced the number of cancer cells and the size of tumors in some patients.

Other treatments using gene-regulating proteins can sometimes convert disease-causing cells into healthy cells. This has been especially successful in research involving liver disease, as the liver is a regenerative organ that is actively engaged in repair.

Chemist Jacqueline Barton (1952–) found that DNA conducts electrical current, except when certain chemicals or mutations are present. Barton is working on ways in which electrical current can be used to scan genes for damage and perhaps even be used in DNA repair for treatment.

Cancer cells develop differently than normal cells. Watch these two videos that show the difference.

PBS cancer cells grow divide

National Cancer Institute normal vs cancer

The knowledge of how cancer develops has helped researchers find ways to slow down and even cure some cancers. Since the mid-1970s, the five-year survival rate for cancer has increased almost 20 percent. Yet cancer still kills more than half a million people in the United States every year.

IMMUNOLOGY

Immunology is a branch of biomedicine that focuses on ways to strengthen the immune system. After finding what causes certain diseases, immunologists create medications, vaccines, and other treatments. These either attack the cause of the disease or strengthen the immune system to better fight the disease.

Severo Ochoa (1905–1993) was a biochemist and molecular biologist who received the 1959 Nobel Prize in Physiology or Medicine for his discovery of an enzyme called polynucleotide phosphorylase. The enzyme's function is to break down RNA. In research, polynucleotide phosphorylase helps scientists understand how hereditary information is translated into enzymes that determine a cell's function and behavior. Ochoa used the enzyme to study how cells behave when a virus is introduced.

When you have a cold or the flu, white blood cells come to the rescue. White bloods cells are like the weapons in a video game, doing their best to zap the bad guys. Your immune system is made up of white blood cells and they are a powerful army doing their best to fight infection.

White blood cells are also known as leukocytes. They make up only about 1 percent of your blood, but they are important in health. White blood cells detect things that shouldn't be in your body, such as viruses, bacteria, and even cells that have mutated. Then, they destroy the invaders.

CHASING BACTERIA

It may look like a video game, but it's really a human cell chasing bacteria in a sea of red blood cells! Watch this video from a 1950s movie by Vanderbilt University scientist David Rogers. The human leukocyte cell in the video is called a neutrophil. It is following Staphylococcus aureus bacteria. Notice how the neutrophil changes shape as it moves through the many red blood cells.

neutrophil chasing bacteria

Like red blood cells, white blood cells are constantly being made in the bone marrow. White blood cells travel through the blood, but live only a day or two—at most, three days. Many things can cause a low count of white blood cells in your body, such as medications, stress, and certain medical conditions. When you have too few white blood cells, you are at greater risk of getting sick.

Much of the time, your white blood cells are enough to keep you healthy. When white bloods cells can't fight bacterial infections, however, they might get help from prescribed antibiotics.

[Antibiotics are helpful only in fighting bacteria. They have no power over viruses.]

Sometimes, the immune system is tricked by certain viruses. For example, a retrovirus tricks a cell into copying the virus's RNA when the cell makes proteins, essentially hiding the virus from the immune system. White blood cells don't know that they need to go to work because they don't know that the virus is there. Anti-viral drugs might work on a virus only when the virus is active. But some viruses lie dormant, or asleep. One of those is HIV.

The cancer cell (white) is being attacked by two cytotoxic T cells (red). This is a natural immune response.

photo credit: Rita Elena Serda

COOL CONCEPT

PS

HIV is the virus that can cause AIDS. It attacks the immune system by infecting a certain type of white blood cell, called the T-cell. Without T-cells, the immune system gets very weak and is unable to fight off other infections. While there is still no cure, scientists have been able to develop medicines known as antiretroviral therapy (ART). This therapy tries to slow the progress of the HIV virus and give the immune system a better chance to fight off infections and cancers.

Adult T-cell leukemia is an aggressive type of blood cancer with a poor prognosis caused by an infection called HTLV-1. To escape detection by the immune system, HTLV-1 integrates with human DNA.

Researchers from Kumamoto University and Imperial College in London have identified a certain protein in the HTLV-1 infection that causes the leukemia. Now, researchers are looking for an effective way to fight and even stop that disease-causing protein. In this way, diseases that used to mean certain death are now being treated in ways that allow the patients to live longer, healthier lives.

FEEDING THE WORLD WITH GENETICALLY MODIFIED ORGANISMS

Approximately 795 million people in the world regularly go hungry. In order to feed everyone, experts at the United Nations say that food production needs to double by 2050. However, climate change, drought, and infestations can destroy crops, which contributes to the food shortage.

Could the answer be genetically modified organisms (GMOs)? Cell scientists have had some success in altering and transferring the DNA from one species to another. This process can produce hardier and more nutritious crops while eliminating genetic diseases. Another phrase for GMOs is "transgenic organisms."

Most of the commercially grown soy, cotton, canola, sugar beets, and corn crops in the United States are genetically modified (GM). Most of India's and China's cotton is GM. More than half of Hawaiian papaya are as well, and the amount of GM squash is also rising.

First introduced in the mid-1990s, GM ingredients are found in many processed foods produced in the United States, such as cooking oils and sweeteners. Chances are that you've eaten GM foods, which have been determined by the Food and Drug Administration to be safe.

[Food producers say that 75 to 80 percent of foods contain genetically modified ingredients.]

However, scientists, governments, and the public disagree on this issue. Polls show that more than twice as many scientists than the general population believe GMOs are safe. Significantly, more food can be produced with the use of GMOs, many of which are modified to resist insects by producing their own pesticides. However, some believe that GMO foods are toxic. Allergic reactions have been reported in livestock. Discussions about laws and labeling are taking place as people face off on the GMO vs. anti-GMO debate.

Inventor Thomas Edison (1847–1931) once said, "The body is a community made up of its innumerable cells or inhabitants." What do you think he meant? Do you agree or disagree with him?

GMO LABELING

In July 2016, Congress passed legislation requiring food packaging to carry a label, symbol, or electronic code if it contains GMOs. Two weeks later, President Barack Obama signed the bill into law. Although you probably see "No GMO" labels in stores now, it will be up to two years before the law is enforced. During this time, the U.S. Department of Agriculture will create guidelines.

Meanwhile, researchers continue to look for solutions. In 2012, a genetic tool called CRISPR-Cas9 was introduced. CRISPR-Cas9 is a technology that allows for easy editing of the genome. It basically introduces a mutation by removing, adding, or altering sections of DNA. The tool promises to be more specific than earlier genetic modifications, with the ability to turn a single gene on or off in plant genetics. Experiments are currently underway.

We have seen cell science make great strides in the past several decades. Scientists are learning more and more about how to manipulate cells and parts of cells to make human lives healthier. What about the future? What do you think the next great discoveries might be?

KEY QUESTIONS

- What is HeLa, and what contribution did it make to cell science?
- What have researchers learned about cancer through cell science?
- Do you think GMOs are beneficial? Do you think they're dangerous? What actions do you think governments should take on GMOs?

YOUR DNA

Almost every cell in your body contains DNA, and 99.9 percent of the DNA between two people is exactly the same. Our differences, what makes each of us unique, are found in that 0.1 percent. What does your DNA look like?

Ideas for Supplies ▼

- disposable cups
- test tubes
- dishwashing soap
- table salt
- cold rubbing alcohol
- small glass or acrylic rod

- **First you need to prepare a test tube to culture your DNA.** Mix 1 part dishwashing soap with 3 parts water. Add 1 teaspoon of the solution to the test tube.

- **Now you can harvest some of your DNA.** Mix a little table salt in 1 cup of water in a cup. Place a mouthful of the saltwater solution in your mouth. Swish it around for 30 seconds. This will loosen some dead cells in the mouth. Spit the saltwater solution from your mouth into a clean paper cup.

- **To culture your DNA, pour approximately 2 teaspoons of your salt water spit into the test tube with the dish soap.** Cap the test tube and gently rock it for a few minutes. Uncap the tube and add 1 teaspoon of the icy rubbing alcohol in the test tube. The alcohol should float above the soapy salt water solution.

- **Now, wait and observe.** Allow the tube to stand for one minute. Using a thin rod, gently move some of the alcohol into the soap. This is where your DNA will most likely lie.

- **To collect the DNA, try to wrap it around the rod.** Scrape the DNA from the rod into a second test tube with a teaspoon of rubbing alcohol. Put a cap on this second test tube. What can you see with just your eyes?

To investigate more, prepare a slide with your sample and look at it with a microscope. What does it look like under magnification? Does it look like you expected it to? Why or why not? Find more DNA experiments at Dolan DNA Learning Laboratory here.

🔍 **DNALC fingerprint lab**

Chapter 7 ▶

The Future of Cell Science

WE'RE CURING SICKNESS AT THE CELLULAR LEVEL!

How can we use our knowledge of cells to treat illness and disease in the future?

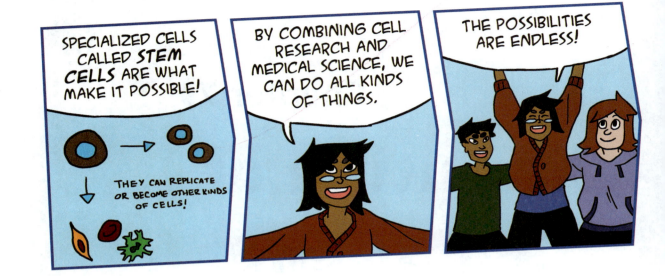

By studying stem cells, scientists are discovering new ways of treating illnesses and injuries to improve the lives and health of millions of people.

Every cell contains in its genes the traits that it displays. Our understanding of our physical selves through cell science has grown, but can cell science tell us about learning, behavior, and personalities?

Cell science in the early twenty-first century has been compared to the space race of the mid-twentieth century. But instead of space travel, now it is the cellular level of ourselves that is being explored. With technology that allows us to sequence the human genome and even alter DNA, who will be next to create something new that benefits the human race?

Advancements in cell science have resulted in new fields that merge biology with technology, medicine, and engineering—biotechnology, biomedicine, and bioengineering. Cell-based therapies are being used to treat disease. These therapies have led to a new category of medicine, called regenerative, or reparative, medicine. And much of it started with stem cells.

STEM CELLS

Every day, people lose limbs, vision, and other abilities. Accidents, viruses, and hereditary conditions are often to blame. In cases of organ failures, transplants are sometimes the answer, but there aren't enough organs available for everyone who needs one. Even when a transplant organ is located, transplantation is major surgery that carries the risk that the body will reject the new organ.

[## What if new organs could be grown?]

What if therapies could be developed that would regenerate, or grow, damaged organs or cells? These things are possible with stem cells.

Stem cells are sometimes called undifferentiated, or immature, cells. They have not yet formed into a fully functional cell. Instead, they can become any type of cell. When introduced to other cells in the body, certain genes in the stem cells are turned off. For example, in the case of a spinal cord injury, putting stem cells in the spinal cord and exposing those cells to the right environment could stimulate those cells to become new neurons.

You can think of stem cells as newborn cells with a seemingly limitless ability to be anything we need them to be. They can help tissue repair itself or grow new tissue. During cell division, stem cells can even develop into other, more specialized cell types.

PRINT AN EAR, PLEASE

Bioprinters print biological tissue with an "ink" of living cells. Bioprinters have already been used to print smaller replicas of tissue for research purposes. Now, scientists are looking at what else specialized bioprinters can do. Perhaps they can be used to make an entire ear, a muscle, a bone, or an organ.

So far, the research is being tested on mice. The key has been to keep the cells of printed structures alive until blood vessels can supply necessary oxygen. Living cells are combined with special hydrogels and plastics that are similar to biological tissues. After transplant, the plastic and gel components fade away as cells develop into new tissue or bone. If it works, transplant organs may be next.

Not all stem cells put into the environment of damaged cells will be turned into fully functional cells. In one study, less than 1 percent of stem cells grew into new cells. But that small percentage of new cell growth was enough to improve functioning. Studies have shown improvement in many experimental situations.

[
Depending on where they are placed, stem cells can transform any cell in the body.
]

As many as 25 percent of people in the world suffer from neurodegenerative disorders, which include epilepsy, Alzheimer's disease, stroke, multiple sclerosis, and Parkinson's disease. Millions more people are affected by injuries to the central nervous system, such as brain and spinal cord injuries. All of these people might be treated through stem cell science in the future.

ETHICS AND CONTROVERSY

Cell science in the twenty-first century carries a certain amount of controversy. President George W. Bush prohibited federal funding on new embryonic stem cell research, calling it the "ethical minefields of science."

Congress passed the Stem Cell Research Enhancement Act in 2004. This act allowed for federal funding for stem cell research from excess embryos donated by fertility clinics. It was the first veto made by President George W. Bush. President Obama lifted restrictions on stem cell funding in 2009.

Research using stem cells, and especially embryonic stem cells, raises ethical and legal issues that aren't easily solved.

What if skin cells could be converted into cells for the heart, liver, kidney, and other parts of the body?

While the rules were being debated in courtrooms and in public opinion, some scientists began looking for other ways to obtain stem cells. Could they develop less controversial stem cells to use for research and treatment? Cloning, for example, can create stem cells.

Another technology involves turning one kind of cell into another. Nobel Prize–winning scientist Shinya Yamanaka (1962–) of Japan experimented first with mice. He was able to make stem cells that could become whatever cells were needed. The technique involves reprogramming adult cells to act like embryonic stem cells. They are called induced pluripotent stem cells (IPS). In late 2007, scientists used Yamanaka's process on human cells. Recently, there has been success in making IPS cells from skin cells. This also is beneficial for cases where new organs might be grown for an individual using their own stem cells, making organ rejection something of the past.

BIOMEDICAL RESEARCH

One out of every four people in the world will suffer from some type of neurodegenerative disorder during their lifetime.

> Parkinson's, Alzheimer's, ALS (also known as Lou Gehrig's disease), and strokes affect the highest number of people. Alzheimer's disease alone affects 37 million people.

The adult central nervous system has limited capacity for self-repair. Transplants aren't an option and the nervous system is not regenerative like other organs and tissue in the body. Mature neurons don't reproduce or regenerate.

SOURCE OF STEM CELLS

Stems cells primarily come from two sources—adults and embryos. Adult stem cells are found in human tissue, such as in the muscle and the pancreas. Neural brain cells can be cultured from adult brains for up to five days after death. But the best source of adult stem cells is the bone marrow. Bone marrow is the spongy tissue inside some bones.

Pluripotent stem cells, which come from embryos, seem to show the most promise. Pro-life advocates object to the use of cells from embryos. The issue speaks to the question of when life begins. It became a hotly contested subject in the 2004 presidential election between George W. Bush and John Kerry.

People with injuries to the nervous system have had limited treatment options, until recently.

The nervous system includes the spinal cord and the brain. Many, but not all, central nervous system conditions hit later in life. However, spinal cord injuries and traumatic brain injuries affect people of all ages.

[About 12,000 people experience a spinal cord injury in the United States every year.]

Unlike broken limbs, broken spinal cords can't be repaired. People who survive spinal cord injuries are sometimes left paralyzed.

According to the Centers for Disease Control and Prevention, traumatic brain injuries (TBIs) affect about 1.7 million people in the United States each year. About 52,000 die, while others are at risk of permanent brain damage.

CHRISTOPHER REEVE

Actor Christopher Reeve, famous for the Superman movies in the late 1970s and 1980, was a victim of a spinal cord injury due to a horseback riding accident. After his injury and until his death in 2004, he encouraged stem cell research.

Actor Christopher Reeve testifying on stem cell research

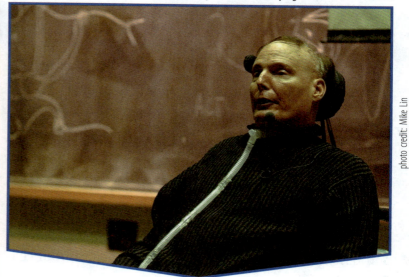

photo credit: Mike Lin

TBIs are the leading cause of death and disability among American youth. The highest rates are among children ages 0 to 4 and adolescents 15 to 19 years old.

Another danger is strokes, which attack the nervous system. Most strokes are ischemic strokes. They happen when blood can't get to the brain because of a blockage, such as a clot. When blood can't get to the brain, neurons die. The first sign of a stroke is often weakness in the arm on one side or one side of the face drooping. Speech can become slurred or even disappear.

Current treatments for stroke can limit the damage, if they are given within a few hours of the stroke. Symptoms of stroke vary, as do symptoms of heart attacks. They are not always obvious, so many people miss their "window of opportunity" for treatment. But stem cell research might be changing the prognosis.

> What would you be willing to do
> if a stroke took away the power
> to walk or feed or dress yourself?
> Would you be willing to have a
> hole drilled in your skull?

Eighteen people did just that when they agreed to be part of a study on treating stroke victims with stem cells at Stanford University. All subjects had experienced a stroke between six months and three years before the study. Scientists have shown that people's brains stop regenerating six months after a stroke. Damage was irreversible because the neurons were dead, just like severed wires in a circuit.

In this study, doctors drilled a hole into each patient's skull and injected donor stem cells around the damaged parts of the brains.

COOL CONCEPT

Do you know someone with heart disease? It is the number one killer in the United States, with one person dying approximately every 34 seconds. For a person with cardiac disease, enough oxygen isn't getting to the heart, which eventually kills heart muscle cells known as cardiomyocytes. Researchers are looking at the possibilities of using stem cells to grow and replace damaged heart tissue.

The stems cells seemed to jumpstart the parts of the brains thought to be dead. The procedure required only local anesthetic so patients were awake during the entire time. They were able to go home the next day.

The results have been remarkable. Functioning was returned to parts of the brain thought to be permanently damaged. People who had been confined to wheelchairs walked again. And even though stem cells don't survive for long in brains, recovery continued even after the stems cells disappeared.

If stem cell treatment can lead to healing in people with spinal cord injuries and damage from stroke, what are the possibilities for other neurodegenerative disorders, including Lou Gehrig's disease and Alzheimer's? Could stem cell treatment make a difference for people such as actor Michael J. Fox, who has Parkinson's disease? What about TBIs that result from near drowning or bicycle accidents? Stem cells could be the future of medicine.

BIOTECHNOLOGY AND BIOENGINEERING

In the biotechnology field, scientists make new products and technologies using cell science. Through biotechnology, treatments and vaccines have been developed that have saved millions of lives.

One example is the development of human hormones, including insulin, which treat people with diabetes. Biotechnology is also being used to create safer medical treatments that have fewer side effects than existing medication and treatments.

Biotechnology is also useful in industry and for the environment. Microbes such as enzymes and yeasts are making manufacturing more environmentally friendly. Biofuels that cut greenhouse gas emissions can reduce reliance on petroleum and help improve our planet's environmental health. Scientists are looking at algae as an alternative to oil, gas, and other petroleum-based technologies. Algae fuel would cost little to make and not harm the environment.

Bioengineering, also known as genetic engineering, uses engineering principles on biological systems. Much of the latest equipment in hospitals comes from bioengineering. X-rays used to be the only way to see inside the human body. Then along came Magnetic Resonance Imaging (MRI), which is widely used in the medical community.

> Biomedicine uses bioimaging, or modern imaging technology, to observe the biological processes of cells, molecules, and tissue.

Bioimaging focuses on not just the structure of the cells, but also the function. Scientists are developing new sensors that can explore structure and function in three or four dimensions.

Bioengineering has also changed lives. People who have lost limbs are using bioengineered prosthetics. These artificial arms and legs allow people who have lost limbs to feed themselves, walk, and even run again. Prosthetic limbs have circuits that remember movements or that can respond to stimuli.

TALE OF A DOLPHIN TAIL

The Dolphin Tale movies are based on the true story of a dolphin named Winter who lost her tail in a crab trap in Cape Canaveral, Florida, in 2005. When Kevin Carroll, a prosthetist, heard about the three-month-old dolphin, he made her a prosthetic tail. Winter lives at the Clearwater Aquarium in Florida. She can be seen with her friend, Hope, in their webcam here.

🔍 Winter Hope Clearwater

3-D printing is changing the prosthetic industry by allowing faster customizing to prosthetic devices— for people and animals.

Bioengineers use elements from electrical, mechanical, and chemical engineering in creating solutions for living systems. Bioengineers are needed in medical, agricultural, computer science, manufacturing, and environmental fields. Cell science technology is impacting all these areas.

While questions about life have been asked since the beginning of human history, cell science is a new frontier in our understanding of life. Only in recent years have the most significant discoveries about cells been made. Yet those discoveries have led to amazing advances in criminology, agriculture, and particularly medicine.

Every day, cell scientists are working to understand more about cells and how they work. No one can predict what the next great discovery will be, nor can we guess at the new technologies and treatments that await us. All we know is that cell science will continue to change lives.

KEY QUESTIONS

- Why are stem cells important? Why is stem cell research controversial?

- What applications do stem cells have for conditions or injuries that affect the nervous system?

- Can you think of a bioengineered tool that can help people overcome injury or illness or disability?

DNA SEQUENCE BRACELET

Remember the DNA model with two strands of DNA? DNA contains a chemical code that guides living organisms. Each strand of DNA is made up of four different bases. There is adenine (A), cytosine (C), guanine (G), and thymine (T). The bases always are paired together on opposite strands of the double helix, A with T and C with G.

- **Research the DNA sequence for a gene of a living organism.** You can find some examples here. your genome

- **Tie a knot at one end of each piece of elastic.** Assign a color to each base.

- **Looking at the sequence, find a bead of that color to add to the elastic of one string.** Add a bead for the matching base on the second string.

- **Continue until you complete the sequence.** Tie the end of each string into a knot. Tie the two strings together at each end of your DNA sequence bracelet.

Ideas for Supplies ▼

- 2 pieces of elastic, each from 10 to 12 inches long
- approximately 44 beads in four different colors

To investigate more, track down the DNA sequence for similar genes in different animals or plants. What is alike and what is different in a similar gene in different species?

Sample DNA Sequences of Genes from yourgenome.org		
Common name	*Scientific name*	*DNA sequence*
Chimpanzee	Pan troglodytes	GTATTTGTGGTAAACCCAGTG
Brown trout	Salmo trutta	TACATCAGCACTAACTCAAGG
Human	Homo sapiens	TCTGAGTTCTTACTTCGAAGG
Butterfly	Danaus plexippus	ATGATCCCGACTATTACTATG
Malayan spitting cobra	Naja sputatrix	AACCGACCGCTGCAACAACTG

DIFFERENTIATED VS. UNDIFFERENTIATED CELLS

Stem cells are currently the superheroes of the cellular world because they appear to have limitless possibilities. This is why they're called undifferentiated cells. Differentiated cells have a specific purpose, such as skeletal muscles that contract. In this activity, create a model to show the importance of stem cells.

- **Through drawings, models, animations, videos, or some other media, show how stem cells can be used in treatment for disease or injury.** Think about the following questions.

  - How do healthy differentiated cells work in a specific system?

  - What happens during disease or injury in a regenerative system?

  - What happens during disease or injury in a non-regenerative system, such as the nervous system?

  - What happens when you introduce undifferentiated cells to a non-regenerative system?

- **Possible resources for your Differentiated vs. Undifferentiated Cells project may include the following.**

 Euro stem cell   FDA stem cells NIH stem cell

To investigate more, design a different way to show how stem cells can regenerate another system, such as joints. Athletes wear out joints due to excessive use, and they might need to get joints such as the knee or hip replaced. This also often happens to older adults as osteoarthritis. Studies are underway to look at stem cells as an alternative treatment for joints that wear out. How would this work?

GLOSSARY

acidic: describes a pH value lower than 7.0.

adenosine triphosphate (ATP): chemical energy that provides energy for cellular work.

aerobic: referring to a cell, organism, or metabolic process that uses oxygen.

agriculture: the study of farming and cultivating land.

algae: photosynthetic aquatic organisms.

allele: a variation of a gene.

amino acid: an organic molecule used by cells to build proteins.

amoeba: a type of one-celled eukaryotic organism.

anaerobic: referring to a cell, organism, or metabolic process that functions without oxygen.

anaphase: a phase of mitosis in which chromosomes have separated and begun to be pulled to opposite poles of the cell.

antibiotic: a medication that kills bacteria, used to cure bacterial infections.

apparatus: equipment used to do a job, like a lab experiment.

apprentice: someone who learns to do a job by working for someone who already does the job.

archaea: a class of unicellular prokaryotes that live in extreme environments.

asexual: in cell science, refers to a type of reproduction using only one parent to produce genetically identical offspring.

astronomy: the study of space, planets, and stars.

atmosphere: the mixture of gases that surrounds a planet.

atom: a single unit of an element.

autotroph: an organism capable of making its own food with inorganic materials and chemical processes.

axon: a long extension from a neuron that carries nerve impulses to target cells.

bacilli: rod-shaped bacteria.

bacteria: single-celled prokaryotic organisms found in soil, water, plants, and animals. They help decay food, and some bacteria are harmful. Singular is bacterium.

BCE: put after a date, BCE stands for Before Common Era and counts down to zero. CE stands for Common Era and counts up from zero. These nonreligious terms correspond to BC and AD. This book was printed in 2017 CE.

binary fission: cell division found in many one-celled organisms.

bioengineering: the use of engineering principles applied to biological function to build devices, tools, or machines for a human need.

biofuel: fuel made up of living matter.

biology: the study of life and living things.

biomedicine: medicine based on the application of the principles of the natural sciences and especially biology and biochemistry.

biopsy: removal of living tissue to examine and learn more about a disease.

biotechnology: the manipulation of living organisms or their components to produce useful products such as pest-resistant crops or drugs.

bond: connection between two or more items.

bone marrow: spongy tissue inside some of your bones. Bone marrow contains stem cells.

botany: the study of plants.

capsule: a slimy layer around the cells of certain bacteria.

carbohydrate: a sugar used by cells for energy.

carbon dioxide: a mixture of carbon and oxygen breathed out by animals and plants and also absorbed by plants.

cell: the most basic part of a living thing. Billions of cells make up a plant or animal, while other organisms are single-celled.

cell cycle: the entire process of growth and division of a cell.

cell line: populations of cells that continue to grow and divide over time.

cell membrane: the thin outer boundary of a cell. Also called the plasma membrane.

cell science: the study of cells. Also called cellular biology.

cell wall: the structure on the outside of bacteria and plant cells.

cellular: having to do with cells.

cellular respiration: the oxidation of organic compounds within cells that produces energy for cellular activity.

centrifuge: a device that rotates at high enough speeds that contents separate according to density.

centriole: small organelles made up of microtubules and found in animal cells. Used in mitosis and meiosis.

GLOSSARY

characteristic: a feature or trait.

chemical: a compound or substance.

chemical energy: energy stored in chemical compounds released by a chemical reaction.

chemical equation: the formula that shows substances and their chemical reaction.

chemistry: the science of the properties of substances and how they interact, combine, and change.

chlorophyll: a group of light-absorbing pigments used in photosynthesis.

chloroplast: an organelle containing chlorophyll used in photosynthesis by plants and some fungi.

chromatid: chromosome copies formed during mitosis.

chromosomes: rodlike structures in the nucleus of most eukaryotic cells that contain DNA.

cilia: structures extending from the surface of eukaryotic cells used to move a cell.

circulatory system: the system of vessels that pump fluids throughout the body. Includes the heart.

classify: to put things in groups based on what they have in common.

climate change: the long-term change in the earth's weather patterns.

cloning: growing an identical plant or animal from the cells of a parent plant or animal.

cocci: spherical bacteria.

codon: the sequence of three nucleotides in mRNA that specify certain amino acids.

collenchyma: elongated plant cells that support a plant.

compound microscope: a microscope with two or more lenses.

controversy: something that causes a lot of argument or disagreement.

criminology: the study of crime and criminals.

crops: plants typically grown for food.

culture: in cell science, a culture is cells that are grown outside of their natural environment.

cyanobacteria: bacteria that use photosynthesis, better known as blue-green algae.

cytokinesis: the division of a cell into two daughter cells at the end of mitosis or meiosis.

cytoplasm: a clear, jellylike material that fills cells and surrounds organelles.

cytoskeleton: the meshwork of proteins connecting to every organelle and every part of the cell membrane.

decay: the breaking down of plant or animal matter by natural causes.

deduction: a conclusion reached by reasoning or evidence.

dehydration: the removal of water.

density: the mass of an object in a specific area of volume of space.

deoxyribose: a sugar used to make DNA.

dermal: of the skin.

dideoxy: chain-elongating inhibitors of DNA polymerase used in DNA sequencing.

differentiation: when the genes in each type of cell are customized to their locations and functions.

diffraction: the bending or spreading of waves around the edge of an object.

diffusion: the spontaneous tendency of a substance to move from a more concentrated to a less concentrated area.

digestive system: the body system responsible for receiving and digesting food, absorbing the nutrients, and eliminating what is not needed.

diploid: a cell containing two sets of chromosomes, one set inherited from each parent.

discrimination: prejudice or different treatment of others based on differences in race, gender, age, etc.

disorder: an unhealthy condition.

division: in cell science, the splitting of a cell used in reproduction.

DNA: deoxyribonucleic acid. The substance found in your cells that carries your genetic information, the "blueprint" of who you are.

dominant: the allele of a gene that is expressed in the phenotype.

dormant: no signs of action or growth, but with the possibility of becoming active again.

double helix: the form or shape of DNA as two strands wound into a spiral shape.

drought: a long period of very dry weather.

edible: able to be eaten without harm.

electrical: energy caused by movement of electrons and protons.

electron microscope: an extremely high-power microscope that focuses an electron beam through a specimen. A transmission electron microscope (TEM) is used to study the internal structure of cells. A scanning electron microscope (SEM) is used for fine details on cell surfaces.

element: in science, a substance that is in its purist form, such as oxygen.

embryo: an organism at its earliest stage of development.

embryology: the study of the earliest stages of development.

embryonic: of the earliest stage of development.

endangered: something that is at risk of becoming extinct or disappearing forever.

endomembrane system: the system of membranes inside and around a eukaryotic cell that are constantly exchanging membrane material.

endoplasmic reticulum: a network of tubules within a eukaryotic cell that is involved in protein and lipid synthesis. May be abbreviated as ER.

endosymbiotic theory: the idea that eukaryotic organisms evolved through symbiotic relationships between cells billions of years ago. Also known as symbiogenesis.

enzyme: a substance that causes chemical reactions to occur.

erosion: the gradual wearing away of the earth's surface, usually by water or wind.

eukaryote: a class of organisms composed of one or more cells that contains a nucleus.

evolution: the gradual change of living things during thousands of years.

evolve: to change slowly.

exonerate: to absolve from blame for a fault or wrongdoing.

extinct: died out or stopped forever.

famine: a serious lack of food, resulting in starvation.

fermentation: the chemical process that turns glucose into alcohol or lactic acid.

fertilization: the union of an egg cell and a sperm cell to create a new organism.

fetus: the human or animal stage before birth.

fiber: a long, thin thread that makes up cloth materials, such as cotton or linen.

fibroblast: a type of cell in loose connective tissue.

filaments: very fine threads.

fission: the act of splitting into parts.

flagella: long structures extending from the surface of a eukaryotic cell that use whip-like movements to move a cell.

fluorescent: bright light as a result of some type of energy.

food chain: an order of animals and plants in which each feeds on the one below it in the chain.

forensic: using science to investigate.

function: a purpose, job, or action.

fungus: an organism that is similar to plants, but has no chlorophyll.

gamete: a specialized cell produced by meiosis, either a sperm cell or an egg cell.

gene mapping: a method used to construct a model of the linear sequence of genes in a chromosome.

gene: a sequence or code of DNA that contains the information for a specific trait.

generation: the average amount of time between the birth of a parent and birth of a child.

genetic marker: a distinct, inheritable indicator.

genetically modified organism (GMO): an organism whose DNA has been modified.

genetics: the study of how personal characteristics are passed from one generation to another through genes.

genome: the total genetic information carried by a cell or organism.

genomics: the analysis of complete genomic sequences from different organisms.

germinate: to grow from seeds or beans, such as shoots or roots.

geyser: a hole in the ground from which hot water and steam shoot up.

glucose: a natural sugar occurring in plants that gives energy to living things.

Golgi apparatus: a cell organelle that tags molecules for specific areas inside or outside of the cell.

GLOSSARY

greenhouse gas: a gas in the atmosphere that traps the sun's heat.

ground tissue: tissue of mostly parenchyma cells in plants.

habitat: the natural area where a plant or animal lives.

haploid: a cell containing only one set of chromosomes, such as a sperm or egg.

hemoglobin: a protein in the blood that carries oxygen.

heredity: the passing of characteristics from one generation to the next.

heterotroph: an organism requiring organic compounds for food.

host: in cell biology, an animal or plant from which a parasite or other organism gets nutrition.

humidity: the amount of moisture in the air.

hydrothermal vent: an opening in the earth's crust with heated, underground water.

hyphae: a filament that makes up the body of a fungus. Sometimes spelled as hypha.

hypothesis: a prediction that can be tested through scientific investigation or experimentation.

imaging: the use of specialized instruments to obtain pictures of the inside of the body.

immune system: the system that protects your body against disease and infection. Includes white blood cells.

in vitro fertilization: a process in which egg cells are fertilized outside of an organism.

infectious: illness that is spread by germs or viruses.

infestation: conditions in which there is an abundance of pests.

inherit: to receive a characteristic or trait from a previous generation.

inorganic: substances not made up of living matter.

interphase: the period of a cell's life when it is growing.

ischemic: a deficiency of blood flow.

kinetic energy: energy caused by movement.

lens: a curved piece of glass that focuses light passing though it to make things look clearer or bigger.

leukocyte: any white blood cell.

life cycle: the growth and changes a living organism goes through from birth to death.

life sciences: the sciences of living organisms and life processes, including zoology, botany, and biology.

lignin: an organic substance that forms woody tissue in plants along with cellulose.

linen: cloth made from the flax plant.

lipid: a key substance in most cell membranes that doesn't mix well with water. Includes fats, oils, sterols, and other fatty acids.

lysosome: a cell organelle that contains digestive enzymes that break down waste material.

macrophage: a type of white blood cell.

magnify: to enlarge.

malaria: a tropical disease received from infected mosquitoes.

mapping: making a representative diagram cataloging the genes and other features of a chromosome.

matter: anything that takes up space and has mass.

meiosis: a special type of cell division that occurs during sexual reproduction of multicellular organisms in eukaryotes.

metabolism: the sum of the chemical processes that occur in living cells.

methane: a colorless, odorless gas that burns easily.

microbe: a living thing too small to be seen without a microscope. Also called a microorganism.

microbiology: the study of microorganisms.

microscope: a scientific instrument with lenses that makes small things appear larger.

microtome: a device used to prepare thin slices of animal cells for viewing under a microscope.

mitochondria: a large organelle with a small amount of DNA that produces energy needed for cellular activities.

mitosis: a type of cell division in eukaryotic cells where the cell and its nucleus is divided into two daughter cells.

mitotic spindle: a group of spindle fibers that divide chromosomes during mitosis. The spindle helps to split the chromosomes from one parent cell into two daughter cells.

molecule: the smallest part of a substance made up of two or more atoms.

multicellular: an organism with two or more cells.

mutation: a permanent, inheritable change in the nucleotide sequence of a chromosome.

myelin: a mixture of proteins and phospholipids that form insulation around many nerve fibers, which increases the speed of nerve impulses.

nanosecond: a billionth of a second.

nervous system: a body system that includes the brain, spinal cord, and nerves.

neurodegenerative: the progressive loss of neurologic functions.

neuron: a type of cell in the nervous system that conducts electrical signals.

neurotransmitter: a chemical messenger that carries signals between neurons.

neutrophil: a white blood cell that cleans a wound.

nitrogen gas: a common colorless, odorless gas that makes up a large portion of the earth's atmosphere.

nociceptor: a sensory nerve cell that responds to damage or possible damage by sending signals to the spinal cord and brain.

nonvascular: relating to plants that do not have a system that conducts water, sap, and nutrients.

nuclear transfer: the introduction of the nucleus from a cell into an egg cell where the nucleus has been removed.

nucleic acid: macromolecules found in all cells that store and express genetic information.

nucleoid: a dense area of DNA in a prokaryotic cell.

nucleoli: specialized structures in the nucleus formed from various chromosomes and active in the synthesis of ribosomes. Singular form is nucleolus.

nucleotide: a molecule containing a sugar ring, phosphate group, and nitrogen-containing base. These make up the building blocks of DNA and RNA.

nucleus: the control center of the cell, containing chromosomes and genetic instructions. Plural is nuclei.

nutrients: substances that help living organisms stay healthy, such as proteins, vitamins, and minerals.

observation: the careful watching of something.

oncogene: a gene involved in transforming cells or inducing cancer.

optical: relating to the science of optics, which is the science of light.

orbit: the path of an object circling another object in space.

organelle: a small intracellular structure that has a distinct function in the cell.

organic: living organisms or coming from living organisms.

organism: any living thing, such as a plant or animal.

osmosis: the movement of water or fluid across a semipermeable membrane from a lesser to a greater concentration. Also called diffusion.

ovary: the part of the plant where seeds are formed or a female reproductive organ that produces egg cells.

oxidation: the loss or transfer of electrons.

oxygen: a colorless gas found in the air, needed by animals to breathe.

paralysis: the loss of the ability to move or feel a part of the body.

paramecium: a single-cell microorganism found in fresh water.

parasite: an organism that gets its food by living on or inside another living organism.

parenchyma: the functional tissue of plants.

pasteurization: a process of heating a liquid to a temperature high enough to kill harmful bacteria.

peripheral: the outer part or edge of something.

peroxisomes: small vesicles found around the cell that break down toxic substances and fatty acids.

phenotype: an observable characteristic, such as eye or hair color or dominant hand use.

philosopher: a person who studies knowledge, truth, and the nature of reality.

photoreceptor: a cell that can detect light.

photosynthesis: a series of reactions that occurs in plants and some bacteria where light energy is used to manufacture carbohydrates from carbon dioxide and water.

physical sciences: the sciences of the physical world, including physics and astronomy.

physics: the study of physical forces, including matter, energy, and motion, and how these forces interact with each other.

GLOSSARY

physiologist: a scientist who studies function in cells, organs, or entire organisms.

pigment: a substance that gives color to something.

pistil: the female part of a flower where seeds are produced.

plasmodesmata: tube-like cell junctions that interconnect in the cytoplasm of plant cells.

plastids: plant organelles, including chloroplasts, that contain pigment or food.

platelet: a tiny, flat cell fragment in the blood that helps blood clot.

pluripotent stem cell: a cell that is capable of becoming any type of cell.

polariton laser: an experimental type of laser that works by tossing photons back and forth between excited molecules.

pollination: the process of carrying pollen from the stamen to the pistil of the same flower or to other flowers; results in fertilization.

prey: an animal that is hunted by another for food.

probability: the likelihood that something is true.

prognosis: a prediction of the likely course of a disease.

prokaryote: a single-cell organism that lacks a nucleus.

prophase: the first stage of mitosis in which duplicated chromosomes condense from chromatin, and the mitotic spindle forms and begins moving the chromosomes toward the center of the cell.

prosthetic: an artificial device that replaces a missing part of the body.

protein: an organic molecule found in all living plants and animals that provides the major structural and functional components of cells.

protists: a group of microbes that includes the protozoans, most algae, and often slime molds.

protoplasts: the contents of a cell within the cell membrane.

protozoa: a microscopic, one-celled animal.

pseudopod: cellular extensions of amoeba used in moving and feeding.

Punnett square: a diagram used to determine probability of an offspring having a particular genotype.

purines: adenine and guanine, the bases found in DNA and RNA.

pyrimidines: two of the bases found in DNA (cytosine and thymine) and RNA (cytosine and uracil).

ratio: a comparison of quantities using division.

recessive: the allele of a gene that is not expressed in the phenotype in the presence of a dominant allele.

red blood cells: specific cells that carry oxygen to all the cells of the body.

regenerate: to regrow new tissue to replace damaged or lost tissue.

replication: making an exact copy of something.

reproduce: to produce offspring.

respiration: the process of utilizing molecular oxygen to produce ATP.

respiratory system: the body system of exchanging gases with the environment. Includes the lungs.

retina: the part of the eye that sends images of things you see to the brain.

retrovirus: a cancer-causing virus in which an RNA virus transcribes its RNA into DNA and then inserts the DNA into a chromosome.

ribonucleic acid (RNA): the molecule produced from DNA used in protein synthesis.

ribose: a sugar used to make RNA.

ribosome: an organelle that is the site of protein synthesis.

saliva: the clear liquid in the mouth that helps you swallow and digest food.

scientific method: the process scientists use to ask questions and do experiments to try to prove their ideas.

sclerenchyma: a type of plant cell that supports plants.

segregation: the process that distributes an equal set of chromosomes to daughter cells during cell division.

sequence: the specific or fixed order to something happening.

sexual: in cell science, a type of reproduction with two parents in which offspring inherit a unique combination of genes from the gametes of the two parents.

simple microscope: a microscope with one lens.

slime mold: a eukaryotic organism that can live as a single cell, but joins together to form multicellular reproductive structures.

species: a group from a genus with shared characteristics.

specimen: a sample of something.

spirilla: spiral-shaped bacteria.

spontaneous generation: an early theory that living organisms could come from nonliving organisms. It was disproven in the nineteenth century.

spore: a plant cell that develops into a new plant. Spores are found in plants that do not flower.

stamen: the male part of a flower that produces pollen.

stem cell: a self-renewing cell that divides to create cells with the potential to become specialized cells.

stomata: openings in the leaves or stems of plants that allow for respiration.

structure: the organization or way something is put together.

symbiotic: having an interdependent relationship.

synthesis: the forming of a more complex substance from simpler ones.

taxonomy: the branch of biology concerned with naming and classifying living organisms.

technology: the use of science and engineering to make things or processes more productive or easier.

telophase: the final stage of mitosis, in which daughter nuclei form at the two poles of a cell. Occurs with cytokinesis.

testes: the male reproductive organ in which sperm is produced.

theory: an unproven idea used to explain something.

thermodynamics: the relationships of energy as they apply to science.

tissue: a group of similar cells that form a part or organ of a multicellular organism.

toxin: a poisonous or harmful substance.

trait: a specific characteristic of an organism determined by genes or the environment.

transcription: the process of making an RNA copy of a gene sequence.

transgenic: refers to plants or animals with cloned genes.

transpiration: the process by which plants give off moisture to the atmosphere.

transplant: a surgical procedure in which a diseased organ is replaced by a healthy one.

traumatic brain injury (TBI): a strong force to the head that causes dysfunction to the brain.

tropical: having to do with the area around the equator.

undifferentiated: having no special structure or function.

unicellular: an organism with one cell.

vaccine: a substance made up of dead or weakened organisms that, when injected, causes an animal to produce antibodies that protect from the disease caused by those organisms.

vacuole: a space in the cytoplasm of a plant cell that contains fluid.

vascular: relating to blood vessels in animals and the system that conducts water, sap, and nutrients in plants.

vesicle: a sac inside a cell used to transport components.

virus: small pieces of nucleic acid and protein that invade host organisms to replicate.

water mold: a living organism found in wet environments. Includes downy mildews and white rusts.

wetland: marshy land where there is a lot of moisture in the soil.

zoology: the study of animals.

zygote: a fertilized egg.

METRIC CONVERSIONS

Use this chart to find the metric equivalents to the English measurements in this activity. If you need to know a half measurement, divide by two. If you need to know twice the measurement, multiply by two.

ENGLISH	METRIC
1 inch	2.5 centimeters
1 foot	30.5 centimeters
1 yard	0.9 meter
1 mile	1.6 kilometers
1 pound	0.5 kilogram
1 teaspoon	5 milliliters
1 tablespoon	15 milliliters
1 cup	237 milliliters

RESOURCES

BOOKS

Cells (The Science of Life) by Duke, Shirley. Minneapolis, MN: Abdo Publishing Co., 2014.

Cell and Microbe Science Fair Projects (Biology Science Projects Using the Scientific Method) by Rainis, Kenneth G. New York: Enslow Publishers, 2010.

Cells (Essential Life Sciences) by Spilsbury, Louise and Richard. Portsmouth, NH: Heinemann, 2013.

Cell Biology: Great Ideas of Science by Stewart, Melissa. Minneapolis, MN: Twenty-First Century Books, 2007.

WEBSITES

johnkyrk.com
Cell Biology Animation

cellsalive.com
Cells Alive!

ncbi.nlm.nih.gov
National Center for Biotechnology Information

genome.gov
National Human Genome Research Institute

smm.org/tissues
Science Museum of Minnesota

stemcells.nih.gov
Stem Cell Information, National Institutes of Health

youtube.com/view_play_list?p=F0701633C91835BF
"How to Sequence a Genome"

QR CODE GLOSSARY

Page 5: loc.gov/search/?q=hooke%2C+robert&fa=contributor%3Ahooke%2C+robert&loclr=blogtea

Page 10: thehomeschoolscientist.com/choosing-a-homeschool-science-microscope

Page 10: wired.com/2011/03/diy-cellphone-microscope

Page 11: youtube.com/watch?v=pBjIYB5Yk2I

Page 17: discovermagazine.com/2011/apr/16-interview-lynn-margulis-not-controversial-right

Page 19: nsf.gov/news/overviews/biology/interactive.jsp

Page 21: exploratorium.edu/imaging_station/students/cell_motility.html

Page 29: itis.gov

Page 31: ucmp.berkeley.edu/bacteria/cyanofr.html

Page 34: youtube.com/watch?v=TdUsyXQ8Wrs

Page 35: youtube.com/watch?v=75k8sqh5tfQ

Page 36: opb.org/television/programs/ofg/segment/oregon-humongous-fungus

Page 38: udel.edu/biology/ketcham/microscope/scope.html

Page 39: fishersci.com/us/en/education-products.html

Page 39: carolina.com

Page 40: pbskids.org/zoom/activities/cafe/breadinabag.html

Page 46: youtube.com/watch?v=LTglday5zak

Page 47: pbs.org/wgbh/nova/nature/photosynthesis.html

Page 57: nikonsmallworld.com/galleries/swim/2016-small-world-in-motion-competition

Page 65: institute.sandiegozoo.org/resources/frozen-zoo%C2%AE

Page 73: dnaftb.org/32/animation.html

Page 78: youtube.com/watch?v=bEFLBf5WEtc

Page 81: genetics.thetech.org/ask/ask363

Page 81: genetics.thetech.org/online-exhibits/what-color-eyes-will-your-children-have

Page 82: cdn.rcsb.org/pdb101/learn/resources/dna-model-2013_2.pdf

Page 82: genomebc.ca/files/4712/7428/4912/6.3.3.11%20Edible%20DNA.pdf

Page 85: youtube.com/watch?v=XRgfLPnGQxE

Page 87: pbslearningmedia.org/resource/tdc02.sci.life.stru.
oncogene/how-cancer-cells-grow-and-divide

Page 87: visuals.nci.nih.gov/details.cfm?imageid=9962

Page 88: embryology.med.unsw.edu.au/embryology/index.
php/Movie_-_Neutrophil_chasing_bacteria

Page 93: labcenter.dnalc.org/labs/dnafingerprintalu/dnafingerprintalu_d.html

Page 103: seewinter.com/animals-exhibits/meet-animals/live-web-cams-0

Page 105: yourgenome.org

Page 106: eurostemcell.org

Page 106: fda.gov/aboutfda/transparency/basics/ucm194655.htm

Page 106: stemcells.nih.gov

INDEX

INDEX

Mendel, Gregor, vi, 71–72
messenger RNA, 21
microbes (see single-
    celled organisms)
microbial mergers, 37
microscopes
    animal cells examined
        under, vi, 56–57
    building, 10–11
    cell structure seen
        under, 16–18
    electron, vii, 17, 57
    history of, vi–vii, 4–5,
        16–17, 56–57
    photography of images
        under, 57
    plant cells examined
        under, vi, 43, 45
    using, 38–39
microtubules, 20, 24
Miescher, Johann
    Friedrich, vi, 18, 73
mitochondria, 19, 20, 47, 61, 76
mitosis, 24, 35, 49, 62–63
molds, 7–8, 33, 34–35, 36
molecules, 18, 21
movement of cells, 21–22,
    31, 33, 36, 46
multicellular organisms.
    See also animal cells;
        humans; plant cells
    cell division in, 22, 24–25
    cell structure and function in,
        15, 16, 18–19, 22, 24–25
    fungi as, 36–37
    history of, 15, 16, 30, 33
muscle cells, 59
mushrooms, 36, 37
myelin, 59

N

nerve cells, 23, 58, 59–60,
    71, 72, 99–102
neurotransmitters, 59
nitrogen, 50
nuclear membrane/
    envelope, 19, 20, 60
nucleoid, 18
nucleolus, 20
nucleotides, 19, 74, 75, 76
nucleus, vi, 15, 18, 19, 20, 36, 76

O

Ochoa, Severo, 88
organelles, 16, 17, 19, 60–61
osmosis, 21, 68
oxygen, 30, 31, 46, 47–48, 51, 59

P

Pasteur, Louis, vi, 7–8, 12
peroxisomes, 61
photoreceptor cells, 60
photosynthesis, vi, 30, 33, 42,
    44, 45, 46, 47–49, 50
plant cells
    collenchyma, 44, 45
    division of, vi, 22, 49
    history of, vi, 42–43, 50
    life cycle of plants, 49
    monocot and dicot, 51
    nonvascular, 43, 50
    parenchyma, 44, 45
    photosynthesis by, vi, 42,
        44, 45, 46, 47–49, 50
    plant tissues, 50
    sclerenchyma, 44, 46
    special characteristics
        of, 50–51
    structure and function of, vi,
        15, 22, 44, 45–47, 49

types of, 43–44
    vascular, 44, 50
plasmodesmata, 46
plastids, 45
platelets, 71
Plummer Cobb, Jewel, 85
polio, 86
pollination, 49, 54
Prakash, Manu, 11
prokaryotes, 15–16, 18, 22, 35
proteins, 17, 18, 19, 20, 21,
    24, 54, 60–61, 87, 102
protists, 15, 29, 33–36, 77
protozoa, 33–34, 35–36
Purkinje, Jan, 57

R

red blood cells, 59, 71
Remak, Robert, vi, 22
respiration, 46. See also
    cellular respiration
rhizobia, 37
ribosomes, 18, 19, 20, 21, 60
RNA, 18, 19, 21, 74, 88, 89
Rockefeller Institute for Medical
    Research, vii, 74, 75
Royal Society of London, 5, 7
Rudolphi, Karl Asmund, 45
Ruska, Ernst, vii

S

Sachs, Julius von, 49
Sanger, Frederick, vii, 78
Saussure, Nicolas-
    Theodore de, 47–48
Schleiden, Matthias Jakob, vi, 8, 57
Schwann, Theodor, vi, 8, 57
science journal, 11
single-celled organisms
    archaea as, vii, 14–15,
        28, 29, 31–32